GW00599311

Wobbly Jelly

A Journey through Cancer

by
Mark Compton

Honeybee Books

Honeybee Books

Published by Honeybee Books
Broadoak, Dorset
www.honeybeebooks.co.uk

Printed in the UK using paper from sustainable sources

ISBN: 978-1-910616-24-6

www.wobbly-jelly.com

markcompton101@gmail.com

Contents

Discovery	Chapter One - Mark	1
	Chapter One - Amanda	14
Orchidectomy	Chapter Two - Mark	18
	Chapter Two - Amanda	31
Results	Chapter Three - Mark	36
	Chapter Three - Amanda	46
Friends View	Plus Three - Pete	51
Chemo 1&2	Chapter Four - Mark	54
	Chapter Four - Amanda	70
Chemo 3&4	Chapter Five - Mark	76
	Chapter Five - Amanda	89
Results	Chapter Six - Mark	97
	Chapter Six - Amanda	105
Lapratomy	Chapter Seven - Mark	111

Wedding   Chapter Eight - Mark   125

Pay Back   Chapter Nine - Mark   136

LE JOG   Chapter Ten - Mark   147

The Final   Chapter Eleven - Mark   159

Chapter One

Mark

"Go to the doctor!"

I knew Amanda was right, but the thought of going to the doctor filled me with dread.
"Go to the doctor!"
There it was again, she wasn't going to take "NO" for an answer.
"Mark, I'm serious . . . you should have these things checked out."

A shooting pain seared through my balls. Like being kicked by an angry horse, right in the groin. "Arghh . . . God that hurt." I rolled over on the bed, temporarily out of action. My right testicle was swollen. It felt as though it was making a bid for freedom and, boy, did I know about it.

Life up to this point had been a bit of a rollercoaster ride with more lows than highs. I had generally held the view that things would always work out fine in the end. So long as I was fit and healthy, I could cope with anything. That theory had got me to the ripe old age of 30 with little to show for my efforts except the battle scars of one divorce and one near-bankruptcy.

It was August bank holiday 1993. I had met Amanda some six months earlier, we were engaged and plans for a summer wedding the following year were well under way. Finding Amanda was the best thing that had happened to me in a long while and to hear the plea in her voice, now, I knew I simply had to swallow that male pride and make the appointment.

"Go to the doctor!"

This was not how I had planned to spend the bank holiday. I had been looking forward to a lazy day in bed with Amanda but that was obviously not going to happen now.

"OK! I'll go to the doctor. I'm sure I've just bruised it or something. I think I might have caught it in bed somehow . . ."

Well, it was the best I could think of at the time. I had no idea what or how I had banged my balls, but I must have done something, somehow, because the pain was crackling through me as I tried to get dressed. Where were those loose fitting trousers? I walked out of the bedroom John Wayne-style, retreating to the sanctuary of the bathroom. Which stretching and deep breathing exercises were best for kick-in-the-ball pain? Would a hot sponge be better? I tried all three, which seemed to relieve the agony for a short while at least. As the shooting pains subsided, a different fear began to rise. I had agreed to go to the doctor and that was now playing on my mind, with thoughts of embarrassing discussions taking over from twisted bollocks syndrome.

I had begun to feel the odd uncomfortable twitch some months earlier but had ignored it in my usual fashion of hoping it would go away. I can't say I had noticed any difference down below, but then again I can't say I'd checked that closely either. Everything was in working order and I had had no complaints. Activity had increased since meeting Amanda and maybe the poor buggers were just overworked? Perhaps they were simply strained or sprained or something. I'm sure it will be all right if we just give them some rest. Maybe stay off the bike for a while. Where are those loose trousers?

After graduating from Portsmouth Poly with a Degree in Economics in the spring of 1984, I had stepped into the real world with no idea of what I wanted to do, or how to get a job. I knew that the best way to make money would be to run my own business, but doing what? I didn't have a clue. I took a job as a management trainee with a major building society and was duly posted to Chesham, in Bucks, where I became the junior member of a three-person team.

It was here I met Kate, my first wife, a feisty bubbly redhead who had just graduated from Nottingham University. Soon Kate got her first job, as a trainee accountant and now we were looking to buy our first house.

Our combined wages were so poor that to be able to buy a house we would have to move. Our choices narrowed down to either Birmingham and the North, or alternatively the South Coast. Having been born in Portsmouth, I preferred the South, and so we set about finding new jobs and a new home.

Kate landed a job as an IT trainer for an accounting software company, through a recruitment agency, Southampton Personnel.
"Why don't you try these guys? They were good for me."
I had had several interviews with no joy, so at this stage anything was worth a shot.
"OK, but I don't know anything about IT."

On our next trip down I went to see the agency, not really expecting a great deal but at least it would stop Kate nagging. Come to think about it, she had been getting more and more intense lately. Kate was a highly-strung girl and often she would get wound up by the slightest thing; regularly her blood would boil as we sat in a traffic jam, she swore and cursed the other drivers. I'm sure I didn't help, as I mostly saw the funny side and would just smile, which drove her insane. Many a time one, or both of us, had got out of the car. But I loved her and could only see the good in her; anyway it was probably just a phase. I was sure she would be calmer once we were settled.

*　*　*

As the interview unfolded and Les, the recruiter, quizzed every aspect of my past life, it began to dawn on me where this was going. So, when Les asked the question: "What sort of work are you looking for?"

My reply was swift and firm: "I'd quite like your job."

"We are recruiting right now, can you come back tomorrow?"

"Certainly . . . what time?"

The next day saw a gruelling two-hour battle of wits between the agency owner and me. The interview ended with the obligatory, "We'll be in touch", and so I left hoping I had done enough.

A week later, I called Les, to be told I was unsuccessful and that they had offered two other people the job. My heart sank; I was back to square one with no fallback plan. My conversations with Kate were becoming one way. I was left in no uncertain terms I had to get a job.

Another week passed and I called Les to chase up progress on other work.

"Hi Les. How are your two new guys doing? Have they started yet?"

"Err . . . well no, actually, one of them hasn't sent his contract back."

"Well, he obviously doesn't want the job and here am I ready to start . . . what are you waiting for?" I couldn't believe my cheek but, hey, if you don't ask you don't get!

"Alright, can you come in for an interview tomorrow?"

Strictly speaking I couldn't. I was sitting in the building society in

Chesham bricking myself that Elaine, the manager, would catch me talking to an agency.

"No problem 10am would be good for me."

"OK, I'll see you at 10."

"Elaine, I need to take tomorrow off."

"You can't take time off at such short notice. Anyway we're really busy right now, so no."

"Sorry, Elaine, I am taking tomorrow off. I'll be back on Friday."

I'm now was praying I would get an offer from the agency, as I was wilfully burning my bridges and was certain I would be lucky not to be fired when I returned on Friday.

At 11.30 I emerged from the offices of Southampton Personnel, my face beaming with a Cheshire cat grin.

"Kate, I've got the job! They want me to start ASAP!"

The following day I walked into the building society with my resignation letter in hand, relieved and excited about starting the next chapter of my life.

Within six months, life had settled down and things were going smoothly. Work was going well and I was enjoying the banter of recruitment. Kate and I were married, we had bought and sold our first house and had moved up to a brand new three-bed semi. We hadn't rowed for some time and the crockery was all in one piece.

As time went by, I enjoyed recruitment more and more and could see that this was a way I could make money and set myself up in business. Towards the end of 1988, there seemed to be moves afoot at Southampton Personnel as the owner introduced a succession of new friends whom he was showing around. It was blindingly obvious he wanted to sell up, which made life a shade uncertain for the rest of us.

Soon I had developed plans with a colleague, John, and by April 1989, with the help of a venture capitalist, we launched our own recruitment agency, Scorpio Recruitment.

John and I had a good working relationship, each recognising the other's strengths and we worked well as a team. We had rented office space in a converted warehouse just off the red-light district of Southampton. It was cheap and we were keen to keep costs down. We didn't plan to be there long.

Each morning as I arrived at the office, John would brain dump his new ideas, thoughts and the actions we needed to attend to, and I would respond with an update on sales activity. We started office life with one desk, one fax machine and two cordless phones, which we would throw across the office to each other depending on who the call was for.

And so it was until one Monday morning in June 1989, when I walked into the office and sat down. John, already there, launched into his morning round-up and had been going for a good 10 minutes before he stopped and looked at me. I was sitting there in a scruffy jumper and jeans, unshaven.

"Kate and I are finished. We're getting a divorce."
"OK." John's response was immediate but considered.

The room fell silent. John began muttering to himself, running through the urgent and important tasks we needed to attend to.
"OK . . . I can handle this end . . . you do what the hell you want to."

I didn't know what I wanted to do. Forty-eight hours earlier, my life had been flowing happily; I had had a wife, a house and a growing business. Now my head was spinning and I could hardly tie my shoelaces.

Over the past year Kate had become increasingly intense, frequently demanding to know where I was, becoming more and more jealous and insecure, questioning me over every conversation with another woman. The plates had flown a few times but she had never actually hit me.

The reality could not have been further from the truth; I was deeply in love with Kate, and would never have betrayed her. It had taken me three attempts to ask her out. As far as I was concerned, I had found the woman I wanted and I wasn't going anywhere. I blindly accepted her for who she was and saw nothing wrong with maintaining separate bank accounts. True, I had been working longer hours, getting the business up and running, but thought nothing of it. Kate had been against Scorpio from the start, as she feared it would fail and that she would have to bail me out.

On the Sunday morning I had gone out for my usual bike ride. I enjoyed this time to clear my head and contemplate life. Feeling jaded, I had returned earlier than expected and was surprised to see a friend's motorbike in the drive. I looked through the living room window to see said friend cavorting with Kate on the floor.

I slumped into the doorway, my heart and head racing. I wanted to burst in and kick ten tons of shit out of the bastard in my house. But I was knackered, so I sat there, filling with rage and anger, summoning up the strength to take action.

Kate realised she had been seen, and now footsteps were rushing to the door. The friend made a hasty exit as we exchanged unpleasantries on the drive. I put my bike away and went inside. Not a word passed between Kate and I. I went upstairs collapsed on the bed with the events of the last five minutes running over and over in my head. In that moment, part of me had been torn out and I was smarting from the pain.

It was over. It was obvious to us both that the marriage was no more. My bubble had burst big time and I began to see Kate in her true colours. I despised what I saw, angry at being taken for such a fool. Kate for her part was not shouting or rowing. We sat down on the sofa and, in a surreal moment of calmness, we began to discuss who should keep what.

The next few weeks were like walking on pins. Kate offered to buy out my half of the house; at least I would have some capital, which would help with the business. Once we agreed on this she wanted me out of the house, threatening to change the locks. So for two more weeks, we exchanged emotional body blows, until finally, I moved out into a rented house.

So there I was, 26, divorce on the way, money in my pocket and a half share in a growing business. But I was not truly happy. Various girlfriends came and went but, deep down, I had been stung badly by Kate and was very much 'damaged goods'.

Scorpio was going well, we had successfully paid off the venture capitalist from our first year of trading and made a profit. Plans to expand were in play and we moved into the ground floor of Cheetah House, in Southampton city centre. We had grown to five staff and business was ticking over nicely. But the economy was getting tougher and some of our competitors were beginning to feel the pinch.

Then we suffered a bizarre chain of events. Our offices were broken into and the thieves stole our safe, which contained all our financial records and two cheques we had not yet paid into the bank. Later, we heard that one of the thieves had broken his foot when, in an attempt to open the safe, his accomplice had dropped it from a balcony and it had landed on his foot – karma in action.

Around the same time we had two further cheques stolen and so now cash flow was beginning to squeak. John and I went without pay expecting the money to be returned, it never was. In a separate event, we took a client to court for non-payment. We won the case and he immediately declared himself bankrupt.

In the delay of reconstructing our records and in the face of strangled cash flow, we missed a payment to the Inland Revenue and before we knew it bailiffs were at our door demanding money or goods. We didn't have the money and had no real means of finding it. A frank conversation with our accountants confirmed the worst and so by 5pm that day Scorpio was placed into receivership.

We made sure the staff were paid properly and walked away. One debt was to come back to haunt me. The finance on John's company car was short by £4k. As joint and several guarantors the finance company could come after either or both of us. As John had no assets and I owned a house, with negative equity, it was me they came after.

For six months I had no money coming in. The benefits I had covered the payments on the credit cards, which had sustained my lifestyle as Scorpio collapsed, and as for the mortgage – well, I reckoned they could wait a while.

Then out of the blue, I got a call from a guy who was looking to set up a recruitment company in Southampton - was I interested in helping him? This would mean working on commission only but I knew it could be done. After six months the new business was up and running and I was back in the chair enjoying work.

Our offices were in the old docks and we would often visit the bars on Town Quay for a drink after work. One day in March 1993, I had gone into the Around the World bar for a swift pint. I pumped two pounds into the fruit machine with no return. I thought to myself, this is not my lucky day. I turned round, looking for somewhere to sit and then I saw her.

Sitting, smiling as our eyes met. I returned the smile and walked over.

"Hi, I was supposed to meet someone here but they haven't turned up yet. My name's Mark."

"Hello Mark, my friends haven't shown up either, I'm Amanda."

"Can I get you a drink?"

"OK, but I can't stay too long."

One drink turned into another, and then into a meal. We just talked and talked and talked. This was amazing, with all the other things going on in my life, I wasn't looking for love but talking with Amanda came so naturally, it was as though we had known each other before and were just catching up on our lives, like old friends. All too soon, the evening came to an end; we said our goodbyes, agreed to go to see a film and swapped phone numbers. I immediately called my good friend Hazel.

"Hazel, I've just met the girl I'm going to spend the rest of my life with."

"The phone number is in the address book under DOCTOR."

"It's all right, I'll do it later."

"Mark! If you don't do it, I will!"

Some people just don't give up, do they? Reluctantly, I dialled as Amanda read out the number.

"It's on answer phone."

Temporary relief as for a moment I didn't have to speak to a real person.

"There's an open surgery between 8:30 and 10:00, I'll go tomorrow."

"Good. Do you want me to come with you?"

Not bloody likely! This was going to be awkward enough showing some doctor my bits. I didn't need the added stress of Amanda being there as well.

"No, I'll be fine. I'll call you and let you know what he says. I'm sure it's nothing serious, just bruised or something."

I was working on the age-old principle; if you tell yourself something often enough then it must be true. Well it worked for me . . . I kept telling myself that, as well.

Deep down, there was a growing doubt in my mind. This wasn't right. More and more frequently, I caught myself and would take a sharp intake of breath. Each time was the same, a searing pain followed by a heavy aching pain that would linger for a while. This was not right, something was clearly amiss; perhaps I should see the doctor. At least that would be an end to it, and Amanda and I could get on with life.

Over the previous couple of years, I had come through some heavy moments, what with moving house five times, changing jobs twice, starting a business, getting divorced, going into receivership, stacking up the debts and finally stabilising my finances. My troubles were not over yet.

After Scorpio, I had built up some mortgage arrears. By Now, I had been paying my mortgage properly for almost a year but the arrears were still outstanding. Out of the blue a letter arrived from the courts. The mortgage company was demanding full repayment of the arrears with immediate effect. Failure to pay would result in repossession. The house was worth less than the original mortgage anyway so now I knew I was in trouble.

Dad came to the rescue; he had recently had a heart attack and was forced to retire early. By lending the money to me, he got a better return and I got to keep the house. All I had to do now was to keep earning in order to pay him back.

Since meeting Amanda we had become inseparable. It was not long before most of my belongings were at her house and it seemed daft to live apart. I moved in and rented out my house, longing for the day house prices would rise and I could get shot of it and all its unhappy memories.

Chapter One

Amanda

Meeting Mark was like no other experience I'd had before, not that he was particularly strange or anything! There was, of course, that first initial physical attraction and a nice smile. That had always been important to me but the fact we were very much at ease immediately, started chatting in an open way and almost had that feeling of having known someone before. It seemed being in the right place at the right time on this evening was to be quite life changing.

Very early on that evening we discovered we had quite a lot in common. We both found the psychic world fascinating and exchanged tales of visits to clairvoyants and mediums. A drink and a chat soon led to Mark suggesting we stay for the evening and have a meal. We went upstairs to the restaurant and were shown to a table for two by the window.

Around The World was a family pub right on the water's edge in Southampton. Perusing the menu, I looked out as dusk was falling and the Isle of Wight ferry was passing by the window. Eat . . . how could I eat? My stomach was full of butterflies and food was the last thing on my mind. I tried to concentrate and choose something light and easy. So I opted for a pasta dish, closed the menu and carried on our conversation.

Conversation flowed easily and the evening soon passed. As we left in the dark that evening and went our separate ways, I remember feeling full of joy and anticipation of our next meeting. We had agreed we would meet again soon and probably go and see a film;

always a safe bet just in case we had worked overtime during our initial meeting and the conversation was in danger of drying up! I couldn't see this happening, but you never know.

I was anxious about jumping headlong into another relationship too quickly. I was 29, rapidly approaching 30, still single and wondering where life was going. I guess by now, like others, I thought I would have met Mr Right, be have settled down and maybe have a child or two, but no.

A few months had passed since I had broken up with Michael, a relationship that had lasted for 7 years!! Looking back this is a period of my life I strangely rarely think about; which is odd because it was the longest relationship I'd ever had. I always knew in my heart this was a relationship that would never really last. We had totally different outlooks on life, different priorities; in fact I do wonder what kept me with him! We had some really nice holidays together, I learnt to ski, which he was passionate about, and I sailed a bit too. But he was always a bit of a bachelor type and to be honest seemed to want me but also an independent life. My mother was never really keen on this one; tolerated it really. I spent my time between living with Mum and spending my weekends with Michael. I always felt uncomfortable about doing this.

Mum and I had shared the large family home since Dad's sudden death at 52, four years earlier. She never expected me to stay at home just to be with her, but I always felt guilty about going away as it was a big isolated house. The relationship with Michael came to a natural and very easy end. I wanted out and so did he but neither of us seemed to want to broach the subject. So one evening we just mutually agreed to call time. We spent the evening reminiscing about old times and having quite a laugh about it. I duly left and returned home feeling much relieved and quite liberated. So there I was, single again at 29 and living at home with my mum.

So, Mark and I were now an item and all was going very nicely. Just before I met Mark I had branched out and bought my first house. A relatively new two-bedroom property in a quiet cul-de-sac and I loved it. Mark was spending more and more time with me and it wasn't long before an overnight bag turned into his entire wardrobe, along with him moving in! It made sense and helped us financially, as we could rent his house out. Those first few months flew by and we were very happy.

Then in the bedroom one morning, I saw Mark grimace. I asked what was wrong. He said he'd got this odd feeling "down there" like he'd bruised himself. I said it was probably that dodgy saddle on his bike but he said: "No, it's been there for a while. "

I stopped dressing.
"What do you mean, a while? How long exactly? Why haven't you mentioned it before?"

He admitted he'd felt it for some time, that he'd hoped it would go away but it was still niggling him. I said it might be a cyst and that he should go and get it checked out by the doctor. "I'm sure it'll be fine," he said. I was never one for just seeing how things go. I was anxious he should get it checked out. If he'd mentioned it, it was clearly worrying him, so I begged: "Please go to the doctor."

Chapter Two

Mark

The waiting room was full, with the usual array of coughs and colds and young children clacking and playing and generally being annoying. Open surgery was on a first-come-first-served basis. Not being a regular, I took 8:30 to mean 8:30 and not 8:00, which explained why there were at least 10 people ahead of me.

I didn't want to be here. I wanted to be at work cutting deals, making placements, making money. At ten minutes a time, I could be here all morning. It was the Tuesday after the bank holiday - I had already lost a day. I crossed my legs, yow! The sharp pain reminded me why I was there.

My mind began to drift, and I started to play mind games, watching the other patients and guessing what was wrong with them. I caught another patient's eye and the flash thought, of "God, I wonder what they think I'm in for?" I looked away, trying to maintain that casual, unflushed look. It wasn't working.

"Mark Compton?"
There was something familiar about the name being called.

"Mark Compton?"
I drew a deep breath, this was it. Standing up, I looked straight ahead and walked gingerly to the doctor's room, knocked and entered. Dr Bamber was your typical Dickensian doctor; he must have been 60 if he was a day. He keenly adopted a forthright, no-nonsense approach to illness that blew away all those namby pamby

"I don't feel very well" types. I was sure I was wasting his time and mine.

"Well young man, what seems to be the trouble?"

A perfectly reasonable question, given the circumstances, that strangely caught me off guard. I had been deliberating exactly how best to broach the subject to the doctor, and had rehearsed several alternative opening lines, all of which had deserted me here, now, in my moment of need.

"How can I help you?"

A full MoT and a certificate declaring good health should do the trick. This is silly . . . I've got to say something.

"I've got a pain in my er," (what were they called?) "bollocks."

"What sort of pain?"
I don't know, you're the bloody doctor. Come on Mark, get a grip!

"It's like I've been kicked or something."

"Have you? Been kicked or something? Played sport? Cricket? Football? Rugby? Caught in a tackle?"

Caught in THE tackle, more like!

"No, no, I do a bit of cycling but otherwise no."

"Right then, let's take a look shall we?"

It was all over very quickly - I dropped my trousers, Dr B squeezed my balls, I screamed - diagnosis over.

"You have a lump in your right testicle. I'm going to refer you to a specialist."

"OK. Is that good or bad?"

Dr B went on to explain that these things were mostly not bad and could be dealt with quite successfully but that the specialist would be able to talk in more detail. He could have been speaking Latin for all I knew, my mind was in relief mode that I had successfully dealt with the doctor, and very soon I could go back to work.

"Thursday, 3pm, at the Royal South Hants. Go to the oncology surgery department and report to reception."

"This Thursday?"

"Yes, this Thursday."
There was no room for manoeuvre. Dr B was clear that an appointment had been made and I was expected to attend.

"OK. Thank you, doctor."

I left the surgery in a bit of a mixed up state. Was this good or bad? Why a specialist and how did I get an appointment so soon? Still, no matter, I guessed the specialist would sort me out and we could put all this behind us.

"I've been referred to a specialist. I've got an appointment for this Thursday."
"That was quick! Did he say what was wrong with you?"
"No, just that I have a lump in my right testicle and that the specialist would be able to tell me more. I don't think it's serious."

"This Thursday? I want to come with you. I'm busy at work but I'll get out of it. What time on Thursday?"

This was still early days in our relationship and while I was warmed by Amanda's concern, I was also still a bit embarrassed by the whole thing. Dr Bamber didn't say it was serious, just that the specialist would tell me more. I was sure it would be OK.

"Don't worry, I'm sure it's nothing serious. I don't mind going on my own."
"Are you sure? I want to come with you."

"Honestly, it's just a specialist bloke who can explain what I've done and most probably will tell me to rest up for a while. I'll tell you what he says when I get home."
"You phone me as soon as you get out. I want to know what's wrong with you."

Thursday came all too quickly. I made my excuses at work, something about a second doctor's appointment for some entirely non-specific ailment that I had no intention of discussing in any detail whatsoever at all.

Hospitals have a certain smell about them, a clinical disinfectant aroma, that is all purveying. I didn't like them at the best of times and this was certainly not the best of times. I found the clinic and duly took a seat and waited my turn. The waiting area was very basic with just a few people there, mostly men. Good, I thought, soon get this all over and I can go home.

At last it was my turn. I walked into the consulting room to be greeted by Dr Mead.

"Come in, I'm Ben Mead. Take a seat, take a seat, just a couple of questions to start."

Ben Mead could only be described as Richard Briers on heat. He spoke in rapid-fire sound bites with great gusto. This doctor clearly enthused about his work with the air of the very best eccentric English boffin. I kept expecting Felicity Kendal to appear as his nurse, but alas it was not to be.

"Right then, let's have you up on the table, take a look at you."

For the second time in a week I was dropping my trousers to let some chap examine my wedding tackle. Not an experience I was particularly keen to get used to and I certainly didn't wish to make a career out of it. Dr Mead, on the other hand, did make a career out of it and it was in his hands that my future now laid.

"Does this hurt?"
"Arrgh!!"

"When did you first notice this?"

I thought about this: "A couple of months, it's got progressively worse over the past few weeks."

My right testicle was swollen, it didn't look much bigger than the left but it was definitely swollen. As Dr Mead pressed the right testicle there was a clearly defined hard area within the ball sack, probably the size of a marble. This hardened lump felt very tender and as he applied pressure the pain increased tenfold.

"Excellent! What you have is a tumour. What we need to do is take a biopsy and determine exactly what you've got in there."

Dr Mead's enthusiasm was perversely reassuring, and the thought of performing a biopsy appeared to fill him with immense joy. I on the other hand hadn't a clue what he was talking about.

"So what does that mean?"

"Well, it's a bit like this. Down there in the testes you essentially have all the elements for creating life. Occasionally these elements are triggered to create their own living thing, which then attaches itself to you. This is a tumour. Now tumours can be benign or malignant but either way we need to remove the lump to find out exactly what it is."

"OK." I was listening but, to be honest, most of this was going over my head. So they wanted to perform a biopsy and to do this they had to remove the lump. It sounded a bit delicate, but if that's what they had to do, then that's what they had to do.

"What we are going to do is called an orchidectomy. Now we can give you a prosthesis if you would prefer, to help save you any embarrassment in the showers or anywhere."

Did I just miss something? What was a prosthesis? And how would that help me in the shower? Did it hold the soap or something?

"Sorry doctor, can we go back a stage, what's a prosthesis?"
"A false testicle, just to even you up."

Is this like having a boob job? Could I have a pair of DD testicles? Hey, hey, then I would be proud in the shower and, yep, I probably could rest the soap on them. Bit impractical in the trouser department, though.

I had clearly missed a vital point in the conversation here. I must have misunderstood what Dr Mead was saying.

"So you want to remove my right testicle?"
"Yes."

For a minute I thought he said yes. Bugger, he did say yes. This man wants to cut my right bollock off!

"Is this necessary?"

"Yes."

"Is it serious?"

"We will be able to tell that after the biopsy."

So he wasn't joking, he may have looked like Richard Briers but this was not The Good Life. And still no sign of Felicity Kendal. A few phone calls later and arrangements were in place.

"So we will admit you to the ward on Monday and operate on Tuesday, you will then need to recuperate for two weeks before you can go back to work."

Two weeks! Monday! I couldn't afford to be off work. I was still on commission only and had a bundle of debts to service. And what do you mean Monday? What happened to waiting lists and there's no rush it's only cosmetic?

The reality of the situation was becoming ever more apparent. I tried to assess my options and think through what I was being told. The information was overwhelming and the decision was a simple one. I took the view that the doctor knows best - that they were generally nice people who only did what they had to do. From this point forward, I was in their hands and would do whatever they asked. Let's face it, they had got me by the balls.

"There's good news and bad news."

"What do you mean?" Amanda seemed more concerned than amused by my opening line.

"Well, the good news is I've got two weeks off work." I drew a deep breath. "The bad news is I have to go into hospital on Monday."

"What do you mean, hospital? What for?"

"An orchidectomy."

"What's an orchidectomy?"

"They want to remove my right testicle."

"Why? What's wrong with it?"

"I've got a lump in it, the doctor thinks it's a tumour. So they need to do a biopsy on the lump to find out what it really is. To do that they have to remove the testicle." It sounded perfectly straightforward if you said it fast enough, in a matter of fact type of way.

Amanda was just standing there ashen-faced, with her eyes welling up. This was too much for me. Since leaving Dr Mead I had simply shut out any emotional response. For me, now, this was just a clinical event that was about to happen. It wasn't really me, this wasn't a physical thing. I wasn't involved. I was just the messenger. The tears began to fall down Amanda's cheeks. We hugged each other tightly, locked into one. By now we were both crying, sobbing, comforting each other. Looking up at each other, then bursting into wave after wave of uncontrolled tears again and again. Like a ride on the big dipper this moment seemed like an eternity.

Several cups of tea and tissues later, we sat down and I explained as best I could what Dr Mead had said, how the tumour could be malignant or benign, how in that area we had all the bits for starting life and that sometimes the bits got together and started their own thing and this caused tumours. Mostly they were just one-offs and didn't lead to anything, but occasionally they could spread, so they needed to nip it in the bud. I laughed as I told Amanda that Dr Mead had offered me a falsie and NO I did not want one! Bizarrely, the thought of losing a testicle didn't faze me, whereas the idea of some lump of plastic inside me was a definite no-no.

On Friday morning, I pulled up in my parking space at work and sat in the car for a while. I wasn't entirely sure what I was going to say but I knew that this was one of those 'fait accompli' moments where the script was already written and my task was to deliver the lines.

"Morning Colin, can I have a word with you in private?" I'm sure he was expecting me to say I had another job. I'd been mysteriously out of the office twice that week and now wanted to speak to him in private.
"Sure."
I walked into his office, closing the door behind me and sat down.

"I have to go into hospital to have an orchidectomy."
"Oh," he paused. "I'm sorry to hear that." A look of relief crossed Colin's face. I hadn't resigned. "What's an orchidectomy?"

"They want to remove my right testicle."

Relief changed to a pained expression as Colin contemplated that thought.
"They've found a lump in my right testicle, so they want to remove it to find out what it is."
"Well I don't know what to say. I know a few chaps who have been through similar stuff, they're all right now. Quite a few sportsmen get lumps in their balls, it's usually nothing serious." Colin was trying to say something, to find the right level of concerned and reassuring, and in doing so was being neither.

"When do you need time off?"
"I go in Monday, they operate on Tuesday, then I'm supposed to have two weeks rest before I come back to work."

"They don't hang about do they? Will you need the full two weeks or could you work from home?" I was touched by Colin's concern to get me working as quickly as possible, obviously a tactic to take my mind off the impending operation. However, as I was still on commission only I had no intention of not working any longer than I had to.

Staying in a hospital overnight would be a new experience for me. As a youngster, I had had various cycle racing accidents that meant trips to casualty for stitches or x-rays, which were always tedious affairs but they had never meant an overnight stay.

Amanda took charge of practical things and before I knew it I had two sets of pyjamas, a dressing gown and a pair of slippers, things I had never worn since childhood and was very unsure about now. Add to that a new toothbrush, razor and wash kit, all I needed was a bunch of grapes and a bottle of Lucozade and I would have the complete set.

Monday morning came and we set off for Southampton General with overnight bag and a sense of uncertainty. The lump in my throat was bigger than the lump in my balls as we walked on to the ward for the first time. Amanda left to go back to work and I settled into my new home. This shouldn't be too bad - the staff were friendly, I had a bed in the corner to crash out on and a wonderful view across Southampton's suburbs. A quick recce to check out the escape routes in case I needed them later and walking towards me, carrier bag in hand, was Amanda's mother, Eileen.

"I've brought you some grapes and a bottle of Lucozade."

Amanda's family come as a complete unit so I shouldn't have been surprised to see Eileen but felt a bit awkward, never being quite certain what the correct response to grapes and Lucozade should be. I would have preferred chocolate and beer.

A succession of nurses and doctors stopped by to weigh me, measure me and explain what was going to happen tomorrow. I wasn't allowed to eat anything after 10pm. Amanda had come back after work and it was now time for her to leave, I wouldn't see her again until after the op. As she left, I sat up in bed and with all the bustle of nurses and patients around me I felt completely alone, a little boy lost, worried and anxious about the events before me.

That night was a restless one. I was hot and stuffy in my new pyjamas, with intermittent coughing and noises breaking the silence. An old man with prostate cancer kept getting out of his bed, pulling off his drips and blundering about the ward in a delirious state until two orderlies tucked and plumbed him back in. His wailing disturbed me as I lay there; thinking over and over again about the operation, the tumour. What would they find? I desperately wanted to just walk out and go home. Why was I in this godforsaken place?

The morning came all too soon as I watched my fellow inmates tucking into breakfast, God, I was hungry. The nurse came by and suggested I might like to have a shower and prepare for the operation to come. What she meant was that I needed to shave my bits so the surgeon could get at them. The shower was warm but the cubicle cramped as I gingerly shaved my balls, watching the hairs wash down the plughole. I began to smile at the absurdity of the situation. Here I was shaving my balls trying not to nick the skin when in a couple of hours some bugger was going to lop one off.

An hour later, the porters collected me and we were off to theatre. Anaesthetists must have the weirdest conversations with patients. I had been given my pre-med tablets and was now on a trolley in the pre-operation theatre. The anaesthetist was trying to find a vein to knock me out whilst I talked about the parallels of vein hunting and worm charming like I knew anything about either. Counting backward from ten, nine, eight . . .

Lemon taste in my mouth, my eyes were open but it was like looking out of a frosted window. Figures were moving around me, a metal tube sucked saliva out of my mouth. I was cuddled up in blankets and bandages and couldn't really move.

"All right my love?" "Are you with us?"

My vision slowly began to clear. I could make out two nurses in blue uniforms busying themselves around the bed. I began to talk but made no sense. The nurse took the lemon stick and metal tube out of my mouth.

"Where am I?" My head was groggy and my body felt like a dead weight.

"You've just come out of theatre dear, you're doing fine, just lie there and rest for a while." Nurse popped the lemon stick back into my mouth before I had a chance to reply. I'd been out for the count for two hours and was struggling to regain my senses. The lemon tasted refreshing so I concentrated on the sensation and slowly the mists disappeared and consciousness returned.

Back on the ward I was keen to investigate the damage. Not much chance of that, my nether regions were mostly bandaged with patches of yellow skin poking out. I felt sore but not really in pain. The surgeon had made an incision on the right hand side just below the 'bikini line' and from there they had 'pulled' the right testicle up and out of the sack. The good news was there shouldn't be any collateral damage to my dangly bits.

"How are you feeling, Mark?" A junior doctor had been despatched to check on my progress.
"OK . . . considering, just a bit tired really."
"Good, well it all went well, and there are no complications so if you are happy in the morning then you can go home."
"When can I get back to work?"

"What sort of work do you do?"

"Office work really, mostly on the telephone."

"Well, you really should rest for a couple of weeks but see how you feel. Once we have the biopsy results back then we will get you in to see Dr Mead."

It had been a long day, and I hadn't slept much the night before. My second night was no exception as I wrestled to find a comfortable position, thoughts in my head running over the events of the day, wondering what I would find, or not find, under the bandages. What complications? What would the biopsy show?

Chapter Two

Amanda

Another August bank holiday was all too soon over, and it was back to the drudgery of work. I was now working at a firm of chartered accountants having been made redundant, along with most others, from the television station that had just lost its franchise. I was like a fish out of water to be honest, but it paid very well and was quite a prestigious position working for two senior partners of the firm. One was very businesslike and to the point, the other very charming and witty. They were both nice in their own way. I was not used to working in a place where the people you worked for were known as Mr Davies or Mr Chambers. What was wrong with Paul and Chris? I don't bow to protocol, I'm afraid, first name terms for me and if they didn't like it they'd soon tell me... they never did!

So off I went for another dull week in the world of figures and clients and Mark went off to wait his turn at the open surgery round at the doctor's. Later That evening after Mark had been seen and explained his troubles to Dr Bamber, he updated me when I got home from work.

"I've been referred to see a specialist at the end of the week," Mark said quite glibly.

"Oh," I said. "That's quick, what do they think it is?"

"There is a lump in my testicle they just want to check out what it might be," he said.

I was worrying, but trying not to let him see my concern. "I'll come with you then."

"No, really, it's fine. I'll just go and see what the outcome is and update you when you get home . . . save you taking any time off work as well."

He seemed adamant, so I didn't push the point and reluctantly agreed he would go alone.

I was worried, of course I was. You don't get a referral with a consultant the same week unless they think it's something significant. But we'd wait and see.

Thursday was upon us before we knew it. I went off to work, as did Mark, and he then went on to his appointment later in the day.

I was home before him and busied myself in the kitchen making a cup of tea and preparing dinner. Mark wasn't far behind me; I heard the front door close, he put his keys and briefcase down and joined me in the kitchen.

We stood facing each other and I didn't have to ask. He was clearly going to tell me.

"OK, do you want the good news or the bad news?"

I felt my heart quicken its pace and began to feel slightly sick.

"Go on."

"Well the good news is I've got a couple of weeks off work and the bad news is I'm going into hospital on Monday."

I felt really sick now and quite cold. I took a deep breath and swallowed . . .

"So what's wrong?"

"They want to remove the lump . . . and my testicle."

My mind was spinning and I was now close to tears, which came quite quickly. We hugged and sat down and talked things through. If anything was going to test our relationship in its early months this was it, but there was never any doubt in my mind that I'd be anything other than 100 per cent supportive.

That weekend we went to visit my mother and gave her the news. She was always good in these circumstances and although she too was clearly worried; was there to give us her support and was already lining up her hospital visits.

Practical things needed to be sorted; a bag packed with hospital necessities. His pyjamas had clearly seen better days so off we went to Marks and Spencer to buy two new pairs, some slippers and a wash bag. We were not sure how long he would actually be in hospital but it's always best to be prepared.

I took the morning off work to take Mark in. We parked the car and walked in together through the array of corridors trying to find the ward where his bed would hopefully be waiting. It's when you walk into these places that you think these kind of things happen to other people, but actually we are those other people. This is us, going through this together.

We found the ward and Mark was shown to his bed, all neatly made and waiting, with his name above it. The normal very small locker for your own home comforts and that was it. We unpacked and I tried to make him as comfortable as possible before I had to leave for work. There were others in the ward, some that had already had surgery and were recovering, and those others were waiting.

The day for Mark was busy with tests and chats from nurses and doctors, telling him about his procedure and trying to put him at his ease. He was due for surgery the next morning so I would return after work to give him some more moral support. I left around 8pm and found my way out through the old part of the hospital, which was pretty dark and dingy. I felt a bit lonely and a little vulnerable going back to the car on my own.

The next day I went straight off to work - to be honest I was worse than useless and my mind certainly wasn't on the job. I was thinking about Mark and wondering when he'd be wheeled down to the operating theatre. Thinking how hungry he must be, not having had anything to eat since the night before, wondering if the doctors had been round yet and wondering if he'd been able to get any sleep with all the distractions of the other patients around him.

As soon as the afternoon arrived, I phone the ward.

"He hasn't come back up yet, try again in about an hour."
I guess he'd gone down later than anticipated. The minutes ticked by as I kept an eye on the clock above my desk. At 3pm sharp I called again.

"I'm just calling to see if Mark Compton has come back up to the ward yet"? I asked.

"Oh yes, he's back and all OK. He's a bit groggy but should be OK by the time you visit this evening."

He didn't seem too bad when I went in; sitting up and feeling OK. A day recovering and making sure he was up to it and then he was able to go home, all done and dusted.

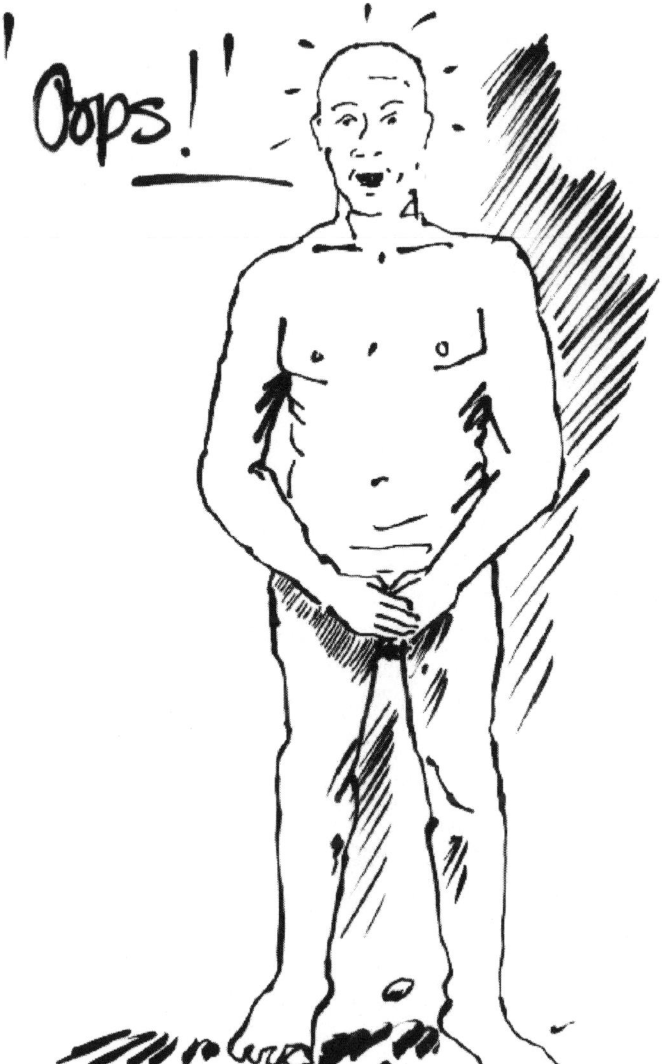
'Oops!'

Chapter Three

Mark

The message on the answer phone was one we were both dreading and wanting at the same time. Amanda heard it first.

"Hello Mr Compton, this is Southampton hospital, we have your test results back, could you please make an appointment to come in and see Dr Mead?"

"Mark, your results are back. We need to see Dr Mead."
Amanda had not come with me on the first visit to Dr Mead and wild horses were not going to stop her coming this time.

The appointment was made and we duly found ourselves in the waiting room of Dr Mead's surgery. This time the atmosphere in the waiting room seemed different.

Before, I was nonchalantly unaware of the other waiting patients but this time I began to dwell on each one, thinking are they in the same position as me? Do they know what's about to happen to them? Do they already know their results? What will my results be? Why couldn't they tell me over the phone?

Amanda sat next to me, pensive and quiet.

"Mark Compton?"

This was it. We were on.

"Hello Mark, sit down, sit down. Right where are we? Ah yes, how are you feeling?"

"Fine, thank you Dr Mead, the soreness has gone and the stitches have now come out."
"Good, good. Right let's take a look at you."

I stepped behind the screen, lowered my trousers and lay down on the bed. Dr Mead checked the surgeon's handiwork, prodded my stomach and tapped on my back.

"Any sharp pains? Or feelings like before?"
"No, I don't really notice it's missing and I haven't had any of the shooting pains or awkwardness I felt before."
"Good, all right, you can sit down again."

I dressed and joined Amanda, sat opposite Dr Mead.

"So how are my results? Is that it over and done with?"
Dr Mead looked at us and smiled in a warm but knowing manner.
"Not so fast, young man."

Ben went on to explain that what I had was a teratoma. As before he expanded on the concept of all the bits for life down there doing their own thing and cited medical stories of people with huge teratoma that had included things such as hair and teeth and all sorts. I think what he was trying to say was that my small marble-sized tumour was fairly insignificant compared to the Guinness book of world-record tumours.

"Now, teratoma in the testes can do one of two things. Either it simply stays where it is or it can spread. Usually, if it's in the right testicle then it may spread to the lumber region. If it's in the left testicle it may spread to the lungs. What you have is a teratoma differentia, which is a variant of teratoma. As this was in your right testicle, we need to do a CT scan of your lumber region to check there isn't any spread."

"Do you think it will have spread?"
"Well, this is why we need to do the CT scan, to find out. Teratoma don't always spread but we need to be sure."

Hmm. For once I was paying attention, and trying to understand what this all meant. On the one hand, Ben wasn't sounding alarmist but on the other hand he wasn't saying everything was hunky dory. I guessed this wasn't over yet and so now we needed this CT scan thingy to confirm the all clear.

The CT scanner is an amazing device. More like something out of Star Trek than 20th century NHS. Having changed into a most unflattering hospital gown and downed my large jug of allegedly blackcurrant-flavoured drink. I was now ready to lie down on the flatbed and enter the giant polo.

From behind their protective screen in the control room next door the nurse explained the routine.
"OK, Mark, what we are going to do is to do one slow pass and then take a number of cross-section shots of your body. All right?"

It seemed straightforward. Why were they talking to me over an intercom from behind three-inch-thick bulletproof glass?

"Now; it's a bit like taking a photo, with a slow shutter speed and we don't want any camera shake, so when I tell you, I want you to breathe in and hold your breath. OK so, breathe in . . . and breathe away."

I had been given my instructions. All I had to do was lie here and hold my breath a bit. The flatbed began to move and I passed through the giant polo. First pass, so far so good. The flatbed moved to a new position.

"Breathe in . . . breathe away."
We moved a millimetre or so.
"Breathe in . . . . . breathe away."
We moved a few more millimetres.
"Breathe in . . . . breathe away."

Now, I thought I was reasonably fit but I was sure I was holding my breath for longer and longer. All this while concentrating on keeping my internal organs still was beginning to get to me. By the end of the session I was literally gasping for breath with my tummy going up and down trying to get all the air back in.

The next few weeks were a bit weird. There was a battle going on in my head. One moment I was dwelling on the events of the past few months, was I lucky to have nipped this in the bud? What if I'd gone to the doctor's sooner? Would I really have gone to the doctors sooner? I doubt it. Truth was, if it wasn't for Amanda I still would not have gone now. Christ, how big would my testicles have to get before I would have had the balls to go of my own accord? Visions of bouncing to the surgery on a space hopper flashed past me. Yep, I had done the right thing.

In the next moment, I was burying all thoughts of illness, blithely ignoring my plight. Phap! It's nothing, just a minor inconvenience. Right then, let's get on with life. What's next? Let's get some deals on the board. I've got debts to service. I've got a life to get on with - or have I? What if it's really bad? What if the tumour has spread? What then? What life? What Amanda? Will she still want me as damaged goods?

With all of this going on in my head, I tried to focus and concentrate on work. One thing was certain; I was earning commission only and had no desire to get back into debt so I needed to work to pay the bills.
"The hospital called . . . we have an appointment to go back to see Dr Mead on Friday."

"OK."

Amanda's news was expected, but I wasn't sure how I felt about this. Before, events had unfolded all so quickly and I hadn't really had time to consider the outcomes and basically went with the flow. This time was different. We both knew there was more at stake and I, for one, had played out over and over again the 'what ifs' in my mind. But despite all this thinking and worrying, and then telling myself there was nothing to worry about, I was still not ready to hear what Dr Mead would have to say.

Our appointment was in a different room this time, this was Ben's office; with piles of notes and books arranged in a neat whirlwind-just-hit style. Amanda and I shuffled in and sat down, nervous, anxious, praying for good news and fearing the worst.

"How are you? Feeling any better? Any worse? Any complications after surgery?" Ben opened with a volley of general medical status-report type questions.

"Fine, no problems since the surgery. Everything seems to be working properly." When do we get to the results bit?

"Any other aches or pains? Backache or neck stiffness?"

"No, generally I've felt fine." When do we get to the results bit?

"Good, good. Well, we have the results back from your CT scan."

At last, the results bit.

"The scan shows that you have three suspect areas toward the base of your spine. This is where we would expect teratoma to spread to from a normal right testicle instance, so we are confident this is spread from your original tumour."

Ben was still talking but my mind was now off on its own journey of understanding. So the tumour had spread. Does this mean it's malignant? Will it just rampage through my body? Am I carrying alien bits within me? How does this happen?

"Had you thought about children?"

Bit of an off-the-wall question. Here we are talking about my spreading tumour and Ben's asking about kids. As Amanda began to answer, the penny dropped.

"We haven't really talked about it. We've only been together nine months and we are planning to get married but neither of us have really said we wanted children."

Amanda and I hadn't really had a full and frank discussion on the subject. Each of us had skirted around the idea but in truth neither of us had said a flat yes, or no. It was still early days and we were enjoying each other without the need for small people at this point and fell into the category of happy-to-reconsider-at-a-later-date.

Ben's point was that there might not be a 'later date'.

"Well, OK, we can come back to that. In order to treat the spread I'm going to put you on a course of chemotherapy. This should have the effect of reducing or dissolving the spread completely. The trouble is that we need to remove the unwanted cells and the best way to do this is with chemotherapy."

Chemotherapy! This is serious. This is what they do to people with Cancer! I thought it was just a tumour, no one said the word Cancer. That can kill you. Throughout all the conversations with Ben not once did he use the word Cancer but here, now, I knew this was truly serious and really for the first time admitted to myself that I was genuinely ill.

"Have you read the book Champion about Bob Champion and Aldaniti? He, too, had testicular cancer, treatment has come a long way since then and things are much better now."

"No, I haven't read the book but I know the gist of it." What did he mean by 'much better now'?

"Chemotherapy can have a number of side effects but the good outweigh the bad. Essentially what happens is that we kill off the dividing cells. Because the tumour has lots of dividing cells, these are destroyed so that it shrivels up and dies.

"The overall effect is that we have to weaken your whole body for this to work properly. So what we do is to administer a course of chemicals, these then attack your dividing cells which will weaken you overall. We then let you recover for two to three weeks to build up your strength and then repeat the exercise. In all we will do this four times over a three-month period."

"So you pump me full of poison, let me recover, then when I'm just about strong enough you do it again . . . four times?"

"It's all controlled but essentially yes.
As I said there are a number of side effects you need to know about. Most people feel sick and nauseous throughout a course of chemo, this is quite normal and we can give you other things for this. Some people lose their hair, but this doesn't happen in all cases. There is also an outside possibility that you could become sterile so, as you have not yet decided about children, we will need to freeze some sperm for you in case you wish to use it later."

Information overload! I'd just stepped into the Rocky Horror Show's day-out at Alton Park. So I'm going to be persistently poisoned for three months, during which time I will be constantly sick and vulnerable to coughs and colds while my hair falls out. Meantime, I have to deposit some sperm at the sperm bank. How the hell do you do that? I'd never thought of sperm as a "might-need-later" type of thing. From what I could remember from 'O' level biology sperm had a pretty short shelf life.

I looked across at Amanda, our eyes said everything and she stretched out her hand. I squeezed her hand so tight and thought I don't ever want to let go.

"We'll make an appointment for you with the sperm bank for next Monday and then we need to start chemo on Tuesday the 28th."

"That's the Tuesday after Christmas. Can't we wait until after the new year?"

"No. You can have Christmas at home but then we need to get on with treatment. You will be in hospital for three days. Then rest for two weeks, and then back in again and so on for four sessions."

We left Ben's office and found ourselves in the hospital café. The hot tea and all-day breakfast could not take our minds off the news we had just received. Sitting opposite each other we held hands across the table, steeling ourselves for the journey to come.

I felt like a complete pillock as I parked in the grounds of St Anne's maternity hospital. What a stupid place to put a sperm bank with all these pregnant women around. I felt desperately sorry for the poor blokes with fertility problems walking into the lion's den with all the potent lions taunting.

"Hi, I'm Mark Compton. I'm here to freeze some sperm."
Not much of a chat-up line but at least the nurse smiled. God this was embarrassing.

"If you would like to take these along to the next room and just bring it back here when you've finished. You should find some material to help you in the cupboard."

The nurse handed me a plastic screw-top jar and a door key. I looked at the jar and smiled. With Jasper Carrott's comedy sketch in mind, I looked back at the nurse.

"Do you want me to fill it?"
"No, just do as much as you can."

The room was much like any two-star hotel room with a bed made up, cupboard in the corner and an en suite. I looked at the bed - this would be so much more fun if Amanda was here.

I checked out the cupboard and found a nondescript box full of 'helpful material'. Feeling somewhat bemused by my situation I got down to the job in hand.

Some 20 minutes later after three valiant efforts the jar was now just about half full. How much is as much as you can? Should I go for a fourth? Could I even if I wanted to? Had I been in here too long? Would the nurse come to check up on me? Well one for the pot should do it.

The nurse looked at the pot and smiled. I was trying to look anywhere but at the nurse.

"Do you want to take a look?"
I'm sure I blushed. "Sorry?"
"At your sperm, under the microscope, some men like to."
"Oh, yes, OK."
So this was what sperm looked like, hundreds of little tadpoles types swimming around with nowhere to go.

"Is that enough or do you need any more?"

"No. That's enough, your count is fine. We will freeze this sample and keep it for 10 years in case you need it. OK, that's it, you can go now." I left the maternity hospital feeling a mixture of relief that this that ordeal was over but anxious about what was to come.

Christmas was a strange affair; my family were spread across the country and it was always an effort to get them together in one place We really only spoke on high days and holidays; in the past it was often me who was the catalyst for a Christmas get-together. Right Now, I was really not in a party mood so was happy for Amanda to take took over.

This was our first Christmas together and Amanda's family were strong on enjoying themselves. Christmas dinner was a major event requiring military precision and firm control of the carrots. With four female members of the same family in one kitchen I was more than happy to keep my head down in the safety zone of the sofa, politely not refusing any drink offered.

As Christmas dinner got under way, I reflected on the events of the passing year. A lot of water had gone under the bridge - I had begun to clear my debts, I had found a true soul mate in Amanda, had my right testicle removed, been diagnosed with teratoma differentia and deposited sperm in a sperm bank. With the smiling, laughing faces of my newfound family enjoying a hearty Christmas dinner, my thoughts turned to the year to come; to chemotherapy, to cancer, to uncertainty.

Chapter Three

Amanda

Life was getting back to normal domesticity. Mark was back at work and recovering from the orchidectomy and seemed relatively good. We'd even managed, one evening, to check out that other parts hadn't been affected!

Then came the call we had been waiting for. I'd got home first and listened to the message on the answer phone. It was the hospital, Mark's test results were back and they wanted him to make an appointment to go back to see his consultant, Ben Mead.

This time I was definitely going with him. Anything that was to be said I needed to hear.

We arrived and took our seats in the waiting room. The waiting time for Dr Mead's clinic was about 30 minutes, which wasn't too bad but any wait is always tedious as time passes so slowly. So, we tried to chat and did our usual trick of people watching. Each time the nurse appeared with a brown file tucked under her arm our ears were poised but again it was someone else's turn.

Eventually a nurse appeared and shouted out "Mark Cumpton please" (I presumed she meant Compton). We glanced at each other, stood up and followed the nurse round to the weigh-in section. This reminded me of a jockey in the weigh-in room having just finished a race - we just needed a whip and a saddle, maybe not! However, this was the first hurdle to the end result of getting through that consulting room door. We were then shown round the corner to a single row of seats in a corridor opposite a whole row of consulting room doors. We took our seats, sat and watched as doors opened and closed. Cups of tea went in and empty cups came out. Nurses came and went.

There were trolleys in the corridor with piles of medical files for people waiting their turn. It was tempting to look for your own and have a quick read, although probably, knowing doctors' writing, impossible to read! Each time a door opened we were hopeful we'd be in next, and at last we were.

This was my first experience of meeting with Ben and I was pleasantly surprised. Ben stood up and shook each of us firmly by the hand. He was a very jovial chap, slightly greying with a bushy moustache. He asked how Mark had been doing and then took him off into a side room to examine him. This was Mark's first visit back since the surgery, so Ben was checking that all was OK. We then sat down and Dr Mead told us where we were now. He explained that Mark had teratoma differentia, a kind of testicular cancer that can remain or can spread.

So, the next stage, to be sure, would be to do a CT scan. I couldn't get over Ben's enthusiasm for his subject. He clearly knew a lot about it and had been to many seminars around the world in his quest to progress research into this disease.

Again I was with Mark for the CT scan appointment. He had to drink a huge jug of liquid beforehand then change into a lovely hospital gown leaving on his own socks which is, of course, just about the most unflattering sight ever! I waited for Mark while others arrived and drank their jugs of liquid before they went in for their scanner session.

Now it was just a waiting game. I thought no news is good news, so I was hoping that things were OK and that we'd get a letter or a phone call to say that there was nothing to report.

We then got the call, it was early December and we were back before in front of Dr Mead on the Friday. From here on in, I was now going on every hospital visit with Mark.

We went in and Ben was his ever jovial self, shook us by the hand and said take a seat. We were in his own office this time, rather than a general consulting room.

Ben told us that the scan had shown that Mark had three small areas near the base of his spine. My head was spinning; this sounded serious. This meant it wasn't just the tumour in the testicle that had been removed, there was more . . . So where did we go now with all this?

My mind was running off on its own course with fears and thoughts of tumours spreading, but I was trying to listen at the same time. Ben spoke quite rapidly at the best of times, so taking everything on board was quite a tricky operation.

He asked us about having children. Had we discussed it? Well, no, we hadn't really. It was early days and we hadn't discussed things further than living together and looking ahead to our wedding the following year. He told Mark he would need to undergo a course of chemotherapy. I was staring out of the window and feeling sick to the pit of my stomach.

I grabbed Mark's hand and squeezed it.
Chemotherapy? This was becoming frightening!
This is really heavy stuff.
Was Mark really seriously ill?

The reality of everything was overwhelming. Ben was suggesting banking some sperm in case the treatment left Mark sterile. Mark seemed to be trying to take all this in, wanting to know exactly what was going to happen to him. I just wanted to say: "Hey, can we stop here just for one moment? I need to take a breath . . . "

Dr Mead proceeded to tell us more about chemotherapy, and the basic side effects. Fortunately, neither of us had known anyone close to us who had been through this, so it was all kind of new. Like Mark, I wanted to know everything we were going to have to deal with. Clearly the one thing most people know about is the hair loss and he said this indeed could happen, along with nausea, the general feeling of tiredness and feeling unwell as the drugs tried to fight the tumours. It all sounded very scary and I didn't like what I was hearing. How would Mark get through this? How would I get Mark through this? All I could see was a tough time ahead but I knew I'd be there for him and we would endeavour to get through this together.

Ben looked down at Mark's file.
"I'd like you in on December 28th for your first treatment."

Somewhere in the midst of all this confusion, I remembered we'd got friends coming down for New Year.

"We can't do that. Surely we can wait till after New Year? We've got friends coming on New Year's Eve."

A firm "No" came from Dr Mead.
"I want him in straight after Christmas."

This clearly wasn't up for discussion. We left the hospital, Mark returned to work and I went back to my office. I walked back to my desk, and my colleague, Tina, came over to ask how we had got on at the hospital. I just looked at her, I couldn't speak, tears were welling up in my eyes and I began to sob. She took me off to a side office and I just cried and told her it was bad news. I hadn't cried at the hospital - I didn't want Mark to see me so upset and worried. The emotions that had built up sitting in Ben's office and in the car journey back were now pouring out. Everyone at work was so nice and supportive that I felt better for being able to release my emotions.

Christmas Day at our family home was a wonderful distraction as we tried as best we could to put to the back of our minds what lay ahead.

Plus Three

Pete

Blimey, this is all a bit of a rum do.

I've known Mark now for a couple of years - he's a nice chap, bit of a quirky sense of humour but his heart's in the right place. It just makes you think, doesn't it? One minute you think you're healthy as Larry the next thing someone tells you you've got cancer! Bloody hell; bit of a shock to the old system. I've got to say; I think he's taking it all rather well. I'm not so sure I could do what he's doing.

I knew a chap a few years back, playing cricket he got hit in the balls, all swelled up and went purple, absolute agony. He couldn't walk straight for weeks! Doesn't compare, though, does it? At least he got to keep his balls, unlike Mark, poor bugger.

Maybe I will just have a check down there, just to make sure - can't be too careful. It just makes you think doesn't it? Having talked with the others I think we are all feeling much the same. "Thank God it wasn't me!"

We were talking about other people we had heard of who had much the same thing. There was that jockey, Bob Champion wasn't there? In fact, I think they made a film about him didn't they? He's all right now, isn't he? Chris said he had a friend of a friend who had had some sort of cancer and he came through it. So I'm sure Mark will get through it, won't he? Still, you never know.

You ask around and everyone seems to know someone who has or has had cancer, yet you don't really think about these things happening to you, do you? I imagine Mark was like that. I mean no one warns you, do they? It's a bit like a car crash isn't it? Bang! It just happens and then you have to deal with the consequences.

Good for him he met Amanda, no telling how long he might have gone before he went to the doctor otherwise. I mean to say, it's not the sort of thing you want to broadcast, is it? "Hello, doc, I've got big bollocks." You never know what's caused it or how it happened, but then that's the point isn't it? If he hadn't gone to the doctor's, God only knows how he might have ended up. No, I'm sure he'll come through, he's made of strong stuff, is Mark.

I don't really know what to say to him. I think it's probably best not to dwell on things, treat him as normal, maybe laugh at those one-liners. What do you say to someone with cancer? Talk about sport, buy him an extra pint, and don't mention testicles. In the pub the other day someone said something, someone else said: "That's bollocks." Everyone went quiet and looked at Mark. "Sorry mate. Another pint?" Still, if the cancer doesn't get him the beer might!

It's just awkward isn't it? He takes it all in his stride, doesn't seem to be bothered by it. I'm sure I couldn't handle it as well as he is. It makes you think, doesn't it?

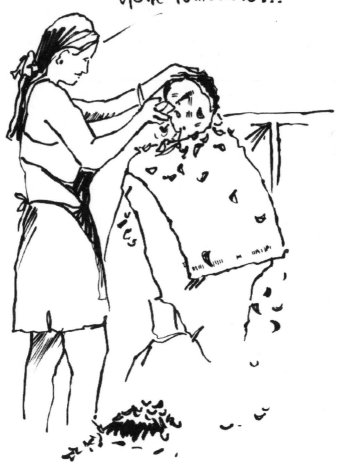

Chapter Four

Mark

"Where are my pyjamas?"
"I don't know, where did you have them last?"
"In hospital."
"They're in the airing cupboard, and don't forget your slippers."

Pyjamas, slippers, dressing gown, I felt like an old git who was about to be put into a home. It wasn't too far from the truth.

Bags packed, we got in the car and set off for the Royal South Hants Hospital. This was session one and, apart from my usual panic over packing, I was deceptively calm. It was only four days before, but Christmas already seemed an age ago as we exited the lift and presented ourselves at the nurses' station on Hamilton Fairly Ward.

"Hi, I'm Mark Compton, I have a reservation."
"Hello Mark, your bed's ready, we just need to take some details first and then I'll show you round."

The nurse checked me in and then walked us through to the ward. The ward was small with one wing covering eight beds, four on each side. Opposite was a private room for the posh people. The loos and washroom were down the corridor, complete with extra wide doors, grab handles and panic alarms. At the other end was a communal room with a TV and the usual array of iffy magazines, jigsaw puzzles and the ubiquitous Connect Four.

"This is your home for the next few days."
Nurse had stopped at the end bed with the ward to my left and the corridor to my right. I parked my bags and sat on the bed.

"What happens next?"
"Well, if you'd like to get into bed, the consultant will be around shortly and he will explain what we are going to do. Then we'll get started. Would you like me to pull the curtains around?"

"Yes, I guess so."
For me, I always felt odd wearing pyjamas at the best of times, but at 10am in a large fairly public room it felt unusual to say the least, these were definitely not the best of times. Nevertheless, I got changed and got into bed. After a heavy session of pillow fluffing I declared myself settled. Amanda kissed me goodbye and I watched her as she disappeared down the corridor and through the doors at the end.

Not a bad pitch, I thought to myself. I could see the nurses' station, with all the bustle of comings and goings. I looked around the ward and began to introduce myself to my fellow in-mates. This was a mixed ward with male and female, as well as old and young. Across the way from me was a young lad in his early 20s. This was his second session of his second course of chemo. He looked drawn and pale and his face told a story of anguish and worry. He wasn't so talkative, so I left him to rest. I felt sorry for the poor lad with his whole life ahead of him, and here he was in the Hamilton Fairly Ward being pumped with poisons. I hoped I would not get as bad as him.

"Mark, isn't it?"
"Yes, good morning, doc. So, how does this work then?"

"Well, what we are going to do is to put you on a course of BEP chemotherapy. This is made up of three different chemicals;

bleomycin, etoposide, and cisplatin. The first is bleomycin, this is the most toxic but don't worry we are only giving you a small dose. Next is etoposide and finally cisplatin, which is essentially platinum, this will leave you with a metallic taste in your mouth.

So how this works is we will put a line into your arm and then pump through the first drug followed by a saline flush, then the second, a saline flush, then the third and so on. We then repeat the process so that you have a series of drugs, each followed by a saline flush, and then you can go home."

"OK."

"Now, there will be several side effects as a result of the drugs, so you need to know what they are and how we deal with them.

"The combination of the drugs is designed to weaken your body by lowering your white cell count. This in turn should starve the tumour. As a consequence, you will feel weak and weary but you will rebuild your strength between sessions.

"Because your body will not be able to fight infection or repair itself as well, you will need to stay away from people with coughs and colds. If you catch a bug then we will wing you back in here to keep an eye on you. You should also use a soft toothbrush and mouthwash, try to keep your mouth clean. Some people lose their sense of taste but this is only temporary."

"Will I still be able to work between sessions?"

"Well you should rest and give your body time to recover between sessions, so you should do as little physical work as possible, but really, if you feel well enough, I can't stop you but I suggest you don't."

The thought of just lying around was not the most compelling, besides which my job was mostly talking to people on the phone and I was still on commission only.

"OK, the biggest thing you will notice is the nausea and vomiting which is caused by the etoposide. Now, we can give you drugs to help with this but the main thing is to stay hydrated, so keep drinking and keep to easy foods such as rice or scrambled egg.

"You may lose your hair, not just on your head, but from all over your body. As your system weakens it stops growing new cells and as hair is constantly growing this is one of the things it stops. We can organise a wig for you if you feel uncomfortable about losing your hair."

People tell you things, describe their holidays, the thrill of a funfair ride or the joy of their child's first smile, you listen politely and nod your head and empathise but have not the first clue of the emotion or feelings they are trying to impart to you. Was this ever the case here and now!

The doctor had dutifully explained all the shortcomings of chemo, all the stuff you need to know on a practical level, but he left me wondering what this journey was going to be like. The vision I had was of diving off the top board and knowing you were going to smack your head on each of the boards below before hitting the water. You knew it was going to hurt but it would be worth it in the end.

By now it was lunchtime. As the practice was to order your 'choice of the day' the day before, I was presented with someone else's parting selection. To this day I have no idea what the main course was. It could have been one of several things. It probably was several things! It was also the last 'tasty meal' I was to have for some time. For pudding I had a small tub of wobbly strawberry jelly, a broad smile beamed across my face at the sight of jelly, memories of children's parties and happy times flooded in. For a brief moment the chemo cloud lifted. If I could have jelly, I could get through this.

"Right then, Mark, we need to put in a cannula and then we can get on with your treatment. What are you like with needles?"

Nurse had laid out a complete sewing kit on the side of the bed. I volunteered my left arm and looked away as she spiked in the cannula. "Yow." A sharp intake of breath. Having foreign bodies jabbed into you, no matter how sharp, is not something you should get used to. Soon there was a line attached and I was now plumbed into my friend the drip feed. From now on whilst we were in hospital, drippy and I would be inseparable. Everywhere I went, he would be there, right by my side.

The first drug was etoposide, and so chemo had begun. I struck up a friendship with Paul, a fellow internee. Paul was on his second round of chemo and he set about passing on the tricks of the trade to me. Filling in all the gaps that the doctors don't tell you. The first, and most important of these, was how to increase the flow rate on the drip feed.

The drip feed was a sensitive device that regulated the speed of the drugs and the saline flush that it pumped into you. If the flow stopped, it would sound an alarm. If it was too fast, it would cause a throbbing pain in the arm. The trick was to up the speed to a tolerable rate, so as to take on board the drugs in the shortest time thus aiming to get out of hospital and back home as quickly as possible. I'm not sure that we ever really got out quicker but it was a great game to play, speeding up the flow, then slowing it back down when the nurses came to check. It did however help us to focus on the job in hand and to pass the time, which dragged terribly.

The evening came all too quick. It had been a busy day, with doctors and nurses coming and going; with new routines and rules to learn and understand and now as I lay in my bed with tubes and lines and plugholes in my body, I struggled to find a comfortable position to try to get some sleep. The bed was hot with starched cotton sheets. I was more catnapping rather than sleeping, uncomfortable and sweaty, my mind anxious about the journey ahead of me, uncertain of my surroundings, not at all relaxed or at peace.

3'o'clock in the morning, there was a kerfuffle next to me. Curtains were drawn, doctors came and went and then the bed with my neighbour of the previous day was wheeled out quietly from behind the curtains and out of the ward.

He was an elderly man who had said little the day before. He had died during the night, and now had been taken away. The thoughts in side my mind cycled through sadness for the old chap and fear for my own predicament . . . would I die? Never!

This was beatable! The state of my ward mates, the young chap in the corner, would he survive? Of the people they leave behind, of Amanda and how lucky I was to have found her. I couldn't sleep, my mind churned over thoughts and fears throughout the night.

Day two and I was already settling into the routine. Little had been said about the empty bed next to me and my mind was filing away the memory deep in a place I would not visit for another 10 years.

Today's cocktail was bleomycin followed by etoposide followed by cisplatin. This was my first encounter with bleomycin; which in hindsight was a draw on points. Bleomycin would win later rounds.

By the end of the day I was tired and weary; the 100-watt bulb inside me was running at 60 watts. I was frustrated by the tubes. I had refused anti sickness tablets - I hated taking tablets for anything, my view was that the less things you put in the less things there are to unbalance the body's own ability to sort out problems. A tad ironic; as here I was being pumped with industrial poisons to sort out what the body clearly had not managed to do for its self.

My chest felt tight, which made breathing uncomfortable. My skin was losing its tone and colour, I generally felt dull but I was determined to speed up the flow and get out of here as quickly as possible.

I slept better that night, my mind too tired to play games. Day three was a better day with just the one session of etoposide to endure; then I could go home and rest, in peace. I had mostly refused the anti-sickness drugs and I felt dull and groggy but not really sick. All in all, I thought this chemo lark isn't that bad, and anyway I'm only on a low dose - it'll be fine. Once I've had a bit of rest I can get back to work and then do this all again in three weeks' time.

"They're here!"

The Pompey Posse were amongst my dearest and closest friends. These were guys I had lived with through thick and thin at Portsmouth Poly and in true soap opera fashion our lives had entwined. So 10 years down the line they were more like family than friends.

"Hi, how are you? You're looking well."
Ann, always was a good liar. Hugs and kisses followed as one by one they trooped in. I had been dozing in a chair but perked up on their arrival, and was pleased to see them.

They had planned to come down earlier but chemo had delayed their visit, so here they were for the weekend. Ann, Andy, Andrew, Jackie, Derek, Sue and their two daughters. This was really only the second time that Amanda had met them all in one place.

Our home was a modern two up two down, so the lounge soon filled up with a play pen in one corner, people sitting around on the floor and music in the background behind the chatter of friends catching up on news.

As the day drew on we had covered most subjects, about who was doing what and with whom. Amanda was playing the first class host, laying on a lunch spread with the help of exotic salads from Jackie. I felt like just one of the gang - nothing special but enjoying the company. In truth, I had hardly moved from my chair all day and by 8pm I was just about done in. The chemo had worked its magic and although I had tolerated the drugs quite well, I had been weakened more than I would admit to myself. I made my excuses and headed for bed. I was asleep before my head hit the pillow.

"They've gone."

"Oh." Disappointment in my voice.

"They stayed for a while after you went to bed but felt it wasn't fair on you to stay for the whole weekend."

"Oh, that's a shame. I'm OK now, it was just a bit of a tiring day yesterday, that's all. I'm fine now."

Truth is I was still tired. I had only been out of hospital 48 hours and my body was just beginning to realise what was happening to it. Pumping in the drugs was only the beginning. Over the following week or so your body begins to shut down as it gets weaker and weaker. The fight back only starts somewhere from day 10 onward and you begin to recover some of your strength. I thought I had coped very well with the first round but I had taken a few more punches than I had realised. In 19 days' time I would be back in hospital for round two.

By the second week I was back into a near-normal routine. I was back at work keeping busy and trying to make some money. My mind was still active but the days were tiring. I had used to be a very light sleeper but now by 9pm I was out like a light.

"Are you ready?"
"Do I have a choice?"
"No. Have you got everything?"
"Yes."
"Come on then . . . let's go."

Amanda was putting her organisational skills to the test by marshalling me into the car on the all-too-familiar journey to Hamilton Fairly Ward. This time around, I was more anxious and uncertain about the events ahead. I thought I had coped well with the first session but knew it would get tougher.

I had a new addition to my kit bag in the form of Basil the lucky reindeer from my friend Hazel. Basil had two fluffy balls hanging around his neck, one red, one green. I wasn't sure if this was meant to comfort me or act as a sick symbolic reminder of what I had already lost. Still I was glad to have him along for the ride.

"Hello, Mark. If you would like to take a seat, we just need to run through a couple of bits and then we'll get you up on to the ward."

I sat down with the nurse and ran through a health check update. "How have you been feeling since your last visit?"

"I've been getting tired more quickly, I've certainly slept a lot more. Otherwise, I feel all right."

"Any nausea, sickness?"
"No."
"Any mouth ulcers?"
"Just a small one but it's not bothering me."

"You need to take care of your mouth, the cells in your mouth are the ones that most easily refresh themselves, so as your body loses the ability to regenerate cells, the mouth can be vulnerable. Keep using the mouthwash and soft toothbrush, it's important to keep your mouth clean."

That told me.

"Any coughing, wheezing or breathing difficulties?"
"No."
"Any loss of hearing?"
"Sorry?"
"No loss of sense of humour, that's good . . . you'll need it."

Amanda gave me a 'Paddington Bear' stare. Well if you take things too seriously you get a headache. I replied with a wry smile.

Back on the ward, I had the 'comfort' of having the same bed as previously. I looked around expecting to see the same bunch as before but this time I was greeted by a new set of faces, each with a story to tell, each worn down by their treatment. David was a bus driver. He, too, had testicular cancer. This was his third session, he was feeling sick and everything was a real struggle. He had been signed of work on full pay for six months, so at least he didn't have to worry about money. Lucky bugger, I had no choice but to work; no work meant no money and I wasn't about to live off Amanda.

"This is Jane, she is a student nurse and she's going to put in your cannula for you. Is that OK?"

"That's fine. Which arm would you like, left or right?"
"We'll have your right, please, Mark."

The two nurses began a 'find the vein' competition on my right forearm, peering and prodding, tapping and flicking. My body instinctively knew what was coming and had taken the view that if they can't find a vein they can't plug me into the drug machine. No veins were to be seen.

"There's one! OK Jane, try that one."

I was trying to be calm but I knew a needle was coming my way and I was still not sure about them. The look on Jane's face told me that she too was not keen on the idea either, she was used to seeing nice healthy throbbing veins; the sort you couldn't miss.

"You'll just feel a slight scratch," Jane smiled in a sweet reassuring nursey style. I looked away and gritted my teeth.

"Yow." The talon of a raging tiger snatched my arm. I looked back, thinking that's over with.

"Mmm . . . I don't think you've got it. We'll need to do that again."

Both Jane and I turned to the senior nurse with a look of fear and dread. I must look after my mouth. I must look after my mouth. All this teeth gritting wasn't doing me any good, perhaps I shouldn't have been so flippant earlier. I must look after my mouth. I must look after my mouth.

"OK. Let's take a look at the left arm. See if we have any better joy."

Joy! Call this joy!

Like a lamb to the slaughter I offered up my left arm, the right one still smarting from the first attempt.

After the third attempt on my left arm, Jane was now more nervous than I was. I kept trying to reassure her that it was fine and not to be put off by my yelps of pain, but my face told another story.

Attempt number four was a success, so at last I was plumbed in and ready to go.

The routine unfolded; pre-hydration followed by etoposide followed by saline followed by cisplatin followed by saline followed by lunch. Etoposide didn't give me a problem but the cisplatin this time round seemed stronger than before. There was now an overwhelming taste of metal in my mouth, followed by waves of feeling a little lightheaded. This was harder work than the first time. The morning session over, I lay down to rest, not really wanting to get up, my mind concentrating on staying focused.

Lunch arrived…. Over the past few weeks I had begun to lose my sense of taste, add to this the effects of the cisplatin and now the shepherd's pie in front of me really didn't appeal. I ate it but felt queasy almost instantly. Perhaps I'll have better luck with the jelly. Yep, that was fine!

"McDonald's or KFC?"

"I don't care, anything with taste will do. I'm starving and I really don't think I can face this food anymore."

The walk down the corridor to the phone was a laborious one, with drippy in tow, but I needed to get word out to Amanda to bring food. I wasn't feeling great and this was just day one of session two. I knew I had to eat to keep my strength up and the hospital food just wasn't doing it.

Like the cavalry coming over the hill just when you're down to your last five rounds of ammunition, Amanda was walking up the corridor, KFC in hand, the smell wafting through the ward. We retreated to the communal room where I tucked into chicken and fries.

"Was that Mary I saw in the corner?"

"Who's Mary?"

"The lady from across the road, I'm sure it was her."

Mary was a lady who lived a few doors down from us. She had a little white bundle of fluff on a lead, which I think was a dog. When Amanda had moved into her house, Mary had been very helpful finding ladders to help us break in after we had locked ourselves out, and sure enough she was now sitting in the far corner, at the bed of her sister-in-law.

"I told you it was Mary, honestly Mark, you're hopeless at times!"
"Amanda? I didn't expect to see you here?"
"Hello Mary, me neither. Mark's in here having chemotherapy. He's on his second session, bearing up well but like a typical man he's complaining about the food."
"Goodness, I had no idea he was ill, poor love." She smiled at me but kept talking to Amanda. "It's a terrible thing, cancer. My sister-in-law has been struggling for some time now. Charlie is devoted to her but there's not much else we can do. We just try to make her as comfortable as possible. She's not as fit and strong as Mark."

We hadn't really discussed my illness with the neighbours, so it was a bit weird to hear myself being talked about with people who knew me. Up to now that sort of conversation was strictly between friends and family.

It had been a difficult day. I was tired and restless, I felt dull and thick-headed but still could not sleep. The bedclothes frustrated me as I tossed and turned, this way then that, tubes and pyjamas, I could not get comfortable. We were given measured amounts of water that we had to drink regularly to keep us hydrated. The downside of which was that we made regular trips to the loo.

It was the early hours of the morning; the ward was mostly dark with the nurses' station dully lit and the night nurses keeping a watchful eye. I struggled out of bed and, with drippy in tow, made my way down to the loo. As I stood there and peed, I felt weaker and weaker as though the strength was pouring out of me. I stopped, and for a moment I thought I might pass out. On my knees, head over the pan, wave after wave of nausea washed over me. I retched and was sick, then again, and again. My head was spinning and throbbing, my eyes awash, my nose running. Retching again and again.

"Are you OK in there?"

It had seemed like an hour but was only a matter of minutes. My head in a fog, I mumbled that I was all right. I wiped my mouth, my eyes and my face and then flushed the loo. Slowly back on to my feet and I unlocked the door.

"How are we doing?"

I felt wretched and awful. This was the first time I had been sick and I knew this was just the start of it. It was comforting to see nurse standing there, watching and caring. She helped me back to the ward, straightened out the bed and helped me back in. I sat up really not wanting to sleep, still jaded by what had just happened.

"OK now? I'll be back in a minute."

Nurse disappeared, to return a few minutes later with two cups of tea. That tea tasted so good, taking away the taste of vomit.
"Thank you, I needed that. God I feel groggy but better now for being sick."

"Good, you should take it easy and try to get some sleep. Your body is having a hard time trying to cope with the chemo. That will take it out of you."

"So is this how it's going to be for the next two months? The first session seemed a doddle. I felt a bit groggy and a bit weak but nothing like this."

"Well, different people react differently. The fact that you came through the first session so well shows you are strong, but each cycle is different and you will get weaker and weaker each time. There's no real way of telling how you are going to be, but you should take the anti-sickness pills, they will help you, and keep drinking the water."

Day two, session two: today's cocktail will be pre-hydration, etoposide, bleomycin, etoposide and, if we're lucky, a dose of cisplatin to finish off. I was still feeling groggy, so mostly took nurse's advice. I was now taking the anti-sickness tablets and trying to rest and catnap throughout the day.

Generally, I felt all right until a couple of hours after my second bout with bleomycin. The primary side effects from bleomycin are tumour pain and fever. Now I felt flulike, cold to touch but sweating, down in the engine room they were shovelling in the coal as fast as they could, I was burning up but had no temperature.

There was no choice but to rest, well at least do nothing more than lie there trying to focus on the good things; on Amanda, on wobbly jelly. Dinner arrived; I ate two mouthfuls and was sick. This wasn't going well. I would have to wait for Amanda and KFC before I could try to eat again. I slept through the night, tired out by the events of the day. Session two was a world apart from session one.

Day three, session two: a better day with just the one dose of etoposide to endure. By lunchtime I was ready to go and called Amanda to come and get me.

I was pleased to see Amanda, now I just wanted to go home.
"Nurse says I can go now. I just need to be signed out and given my going-home pack of anti-sickness pills, mouthwash and assorted other stuff. Shouldn't be long . . . are you OK?"

Amanda sat down by my side; her eyes were welling up. As I looked at her I could feel the sadness, she leant over hugging me hard as she burst into tears. We just hugged and hugged.

"It's all right, it's just chemo. I know it's hard but we'll get through it. I love you, I love you lots."

"I'd be lost without you. I love you so much."

"It's OK. I love you too, I'm not going anywhere."

"I just met Mary in the corridor. Her sister-in-law died last night."

Chapter Four

Amanda

Back at home, with Christmas festivities over we got minds focused on Mark and what we had to do. We assembled the hospital kit again; freshly washed pyjamas, wash kit, books and magazines. He'd be in for a few days, so he'd need things to help pass the time.

This time we were off to the Royal South Hants Hospital, not far from work so I could easily visit in the lunch hour and get back quickly after work. We went up in a very large lift to Hamilton Fairley Ward, a specialist cancer ward. I was immediately struck by the higher level of comfort; the smaller wards, nicer curtains, duvet covers and more home comforts. We had a look around. There was a television room with a selection of differently coloured hard-looking armchairs, a communal area with a fridge, a large table with chairs around and an array of things to keep people occupied - magazines, cards, board games and jigsaw puzzles.

A nurse then showed us to the bed that would be Mark's home for the next few days. We unpacked his bag and put things in the bedside locker. Mark changed into his pyjamas and got into bed to await visits from various medical staff and to get him started on his first treatment. I was nervous for him, anxious about the treatment ahead and couldn't imagine how anxious he must be was feeling at this moment.

However, we always seemed to find humour in most things, so could always have a laugh about the circumstances we found ourselves in.

I think you have to have a slightly dark sense of humour during these times; it helps to get you through.

As doctors and nurses started to appear, I thought it best to leave them to their job. I kissed Mark goodbye, wished him luck and told him I'd see him later. I hated going but I couldn't take all the time off work that I would have liked. I thought it better to take time off when he would need me more when he was back home.

So, I left the professionals to it and felt confident I was leaving him in safe hands. Glancing back and seeing him sitting up in bed in his pyjamas, waiting for things to be done to him, I thought how vulnerable he looked and I felt very sad.

I was out my office as soon as I could that evening and went straight to the hospital. Mark was in the same bed, this time rigged up to a machine with a tube in his arm and a drip with a bag hanging down from it. He didn't seem too bad, said it had gone OK and that he had been given the first drug and was now being flushed through with a bag of saline.

There were clearly people in here in a worse state than Mark. I really felt for what they must be going through. Eight o'clock was cut-off time, so I gathered my things and made my way out through the corridors, back down in the large lift and back to the car.

The next day at work was a long one. I couldn't wait to get to the hospital to see Mark. I knew his days were long and having visitors broke up the day for him. I'd also got my mother going in to visit during the day and take him anything he needed.

As I arrived I noticed the bed beside Mark was empty.
"Has he gone home?"

Mark took a deep breath and said: "No, he died in the night."

"Oh God," I said. I didn't mean to seem shocked but I was shocked. The night before he'd been lying in the next bed and now he was gone.

After day two of treatment Mark did seem to be suffering a bit. He was very hot, a side effect of that day's drugs - his face looked hot and flushed. The rest of him, though, looked paler than I'd remembered.

So, by the end of day three Mark was done. Session one was over. He was unplugged from his drip, dispatched with some anti-sickness drugs and we were off. He clearly couldn't wait to get home.

The friends we had coming down for New Year did make the trip down regardless that week. It was good to see them and I had got plenty of food in. We had a lovely day with them and I'd cooked a meal, which we all sat round and enjoyed.

Mark sat in the armchair most of the day and by early evening he was clearly struggling.
"I think I'll go up," he said.
"OK, that's fine. Don't worry, you get some rest."

I helped Mark upstairs and put him to bed. When I came back down, Ann followed me into the kitchen. "Look, don't be offended but we're not going to stay the night. Mark clearly needs rest right now, not a house full of people. So we'll leave you to it and see you again another time."

I was, to be truthful, somewhat relieved. Things up to now had taken their toll and I, too, was pretty exhausted. Entertaining for a couple of days wasn't really what I wanted to do. So we spent the next few days quietly at home and Mark began to realise that what in hospital he had thought was a "doddle" with round one, was beginning to hit him and was going to take a much greater toll.

After a week or two, Mark was able to get back to work, which was good but he did find found the days tiring and was often in bed early to try to regain some strength.

Before we knew it, session two was fast approaching. We kind of knew the arrival routine now, so off we went to see our friends at Hamilton Fairley. We packed his essentials, including this time his little furry friend Basil, a Christmas reindeer from our good friend Hazel who had been in to visit Mark during session one. We settled Mark in. He was questioned about how he'd been since the first treatment and was shown to the same bed as before, which was comforting as you kind of feel more at home if that's possible!

I was back at work when I got a call from Mark.

"I need you to bring me in some lunch."

"What? Why? Aren't they feeding you?"

"Yes but I can't eat it. It's awful stuff and it's making me feel worse. Anything will do, a Big Mac or KFC would be fine."

I left the office and drove to the nearest KFC, got us both some lunch and arrived on the ward. I felt guilty smuggling food in, but it's what he wanted and if he felt it would help, that's what he would get. Mark climbed out of bed and put his dressing gown on and the three of us, including "drippy", walked down to the day room. We sat and ate our lunch and he seemed better once he had some food inside him.

I had to go back to work and left Mark to his afternoon. Just as I was leaving I saw a familiar face.

"Mary?" The woman turned to me and sure enough it was our neighbour from Brookside Close.

"Hello," she said. "What are you doing here?"
"I've just left Mark in bed. He's having chemotherapy."
"Oh, goodness, I had no idea. What is wrong?"

I gave her a brief outline. It seemed funny that we'd been going through something fairly traumatic and even our neighbours were completely unaware. Mary was a lovely lady who lived on her own with her little dog. She'd been very friendly when I'd moved in. Mary was there visiting her sister-in-law, who was also having treatment, and was now in Mark's ward opposite and kind of over in the corner. When Mary's brother, Charlie, visited, of course, I recognised him, too. We both left each other to our own visiting times but always said goodbye when visiting was over.

Taking food in for Mark was now becoming a regular occurrence. He just couldn't tolerate the hospital food and, frankly, having seen it how could that food boost anyone when they were sick?

Day two of session two was clearly beginning to take its toll. This was far different from the "doddle" of session one. The build-up of the various drugs were clearly having a big effect. It didn't make sense that the drugs being pumped into him were supposed to be making him well but actually he was becoming sicker and sicker. I felt pretty helpless. There was little I could do except give him what he wanted; some tasty food and some company.

As I left for work at the start of day three, Mary was outside her house. Sadly she told me that her sister-in-law had died. This was in my mind all day and so I was relieved to get the call to say Mark was ready to leave and could go home. And sure enough when I arrived he was sitting on his bed in his going-home clothes, bag packed, all ready to go. Why did I get the feeling he was desperate to go home!

We had a brown bag full of various pills and potions to get him through the "recovery" time at home and a cardboard sick bowl for the journey home, which fortunately we didn't need to use!

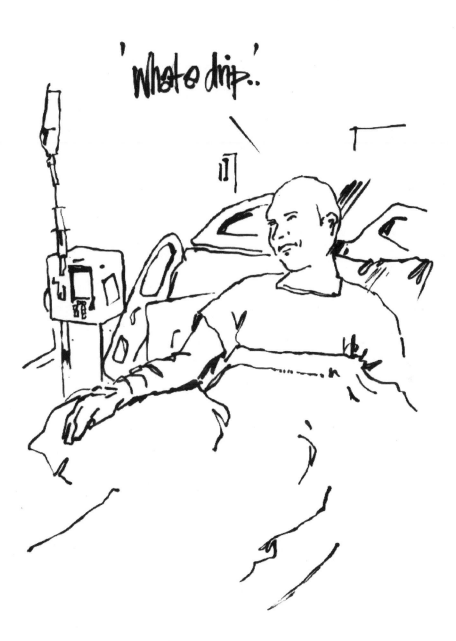

Chapter Five

Mark

The first few days back at home after session two were very difficult. I was used to being quite lively, and expected to pick up where I had left off. With money being tight I was looking to get back to work as soon as possible. Instead, I felt dull and slow, climbing the stairs was taking longer and longer. I would park myself in a chair with a video on and not really move for hours. My mind was still active but my body was on a severe go-slow.

The nausea was getting worse. Every three to four hours the feeling of wanting to be sick would wash over me, sometimes passing and sometimes I would throw up. These were the worst days so far and my bravado after round one seemed a distant cousin to the gaunt drawn guy who looked back at me in the mirror. What I ate was now becoming a major issue, and Amanda was seriously challenged in the kitchen to find food that was easy on the stomach and that I could actually taste.

"Do you want the scrambled egg or just the long grain rice?"
"Neither. I'm not really hungry. Think I'll have a shower first to wake me up and hopefully make me feel a bit better."
"All right but don't have it too hot!"

I trudged upstairs and got into the shower. The warm water felt soothing as I lathered away with the shower gel. Stepping out I looked back at the shower tray. Each time I washed, every night I slept, a few more hairs would fall out. I was thinning nicely but still had enough to warrant a comb. As I dried myself off and gently patted my hair not wanting to rub it too vigorously, clumps of hair came away in my hand.

"Amanda . . . can you come up a minute?"
"I'm cooking. What is it?"
"Can you just come up, please?"

Thud thud thud, as Amanda came upstairs, 10 times faster than I could. She stood in the bathroom doorway, absorbing the pathetic view of me standing there with clumps of hair in my hand.

"Oh, my God."
"I don't think much of that shampoo!"

I ran my hands through my hair a few more times, there were now patches of scalp showing through.

"I think it's clipper time. Just tidy it up a bit."

Amanda found the clippers and set to, taking out the thin bits. After the best part of half an hour, with me directing, twisting my head this way then that, trying to look in mirrors reflecting mirrors, all the time Amanda trying to take artistic control, clipping and tweaking, I was left with a bald top and neatly pruned side borders. I looked like a cross between a poodle and Coco the Clown.

My eyes flitted from the mirror then back to Amanda, then back in the mirror again then back to Amanda. By this time she was struggling to keep a straight face and could hold it no longer. She burst into tears of laughter, grinning from ear to ear.
"It's not funny!" I protested, with an equally ridiculous grin. "It's got to go!"
"What? All of it?"
"Yep, it's going to fall out sooner or later, so it might as well be now. Get it over and done with."

OK, I think it's for the best."

With that Amanda took the clippers to what was left of my hair and a whole new world opened up for Mark the skinhead.

That night as I got into bed, the sensation of bald head against pillow unnerved me for a second, my head felt cold and vulnerable, my mind drifted to thoughts of my own vulnerability. I need to be strong, I need to get through this, this will pass. I feel lightheaded - I'm going to be sick.

By the end of week three, I still felt jaded but the sickness had passed. We were now into February and session three was beckoning.

"Where's my cap?"
"Which one?"
"The one Sue bought me in Worcester."

The winter air was fresh, to say the least, and I was still getting used to the hair-free lifestyle. Still, I was now the proud owner of a selection of hats, most of which simply slipped off my head in the slightest breeze.

"You're very quiet, come on, you'll be fine." Amanda was doing a good job trying to reassure me. Truth was, I was still tired from the last session and didn't feel as strong or as ready for this as I would have liked.
"Yeah, you're right. I'm fine honestly, just keep bringing the KFC. I hope there's jelly for tea."

As we made our way on to Hamilton Fairley Ward, pushing open the swing doors, I could hear the seconds ringing the bell and calling "Round three, Compo versus chemo, one round all". I was damned certain I was going to come out fighting.

"Morning, Mark. A bit of a change since your last visit."

"Hi, yes. I thought I'd dye it transparent. What do you think?"

"I think it suits you but if you like I can arrange for a wig specialist to come and see you. Men don't always want a wig. I think for them being bald is a bit of a statement. It tends to be the women who don't get on so well. It's not really socially acceptable for women to be bald, so they usually prefer to wear a wig."

Amanda and nurse empathised at the thought of being bald.

"Is it free?"

"Yes, it's all part of the service."

"OK, why not? It could be a bit of a laugh."

"All right then, I'll sort that out for you. You seem to be in good spirits, how have you been since last time?"

"Not great to be honest, I'm just feeling more tired. At the start I was being sick three or four times a day but that has now improved. I was getting chest pains lying down, I'm not sure if that was just being sore from vomiting or something else. My taste buds have turned the volume down, but mostly I just feel tired all the time."

"OK, the chest pain may be caused by the cisplatin. We'll do a chest x-ray to check. The rest of it is pretty much as we would expect. Are you ready to go on to the ward?"

"Guess so, the sooner we get started, the sooner I can go home again."

This time around I was stationed in a middle bed on the left hand side. I mentally noted that I hadn't seen anyone die in this slot, which was good. Again, the faces around me were all new. I was hoping to see someone familiar, someone I could swap notes with, or debrief on what I could really expect this time round.

Amanda made sure I was comfortable, then kissed me goodbye and disappeared down the end of the corridor. Her leaving always made me sad. I was only just beginning to understand how much

I relied upon her, how much I truly loved her, how much I needed her to be strong.

Round three and the routine would be much the same, pre-hydration followed by etoposide, followed by saline followed by cisplatin followed by saline followed by bleomycin. Lunch came round and I sat up in bed and looked forlornly at the meal in front of me. I didn't touch it, I couldn't touch it, the sight and smell of it made me feel sick and this was day one. I tried to listen to music or watch the TV but for most of the time I just lay down, resting. I really didn't feel like talking much to the other patients.

Time dragged, as I waited for Amanda's next visit, hoping she would bring food. My whole day was filled with making sure I drank enough water, making sure I peed enough, feeling sick, being sick. Minutes felt like hours, hours felt like days. I would close my eyes and try to count a minute; the closest I got was 45 seconds.

Day two session three, and I was feeling brighter. I was still weary from being sick but my head was clearer. Today's special was a double dose of cisplatin and a dose of bleomycin. The ward seemed more purposeful today, with lots of bustle. I sat up in bed and took in the comings and goings.

On the previous two visits, I had felt like part of the ward, more the centre of attention. This time round I felt more like an observer, watching a play unfold in front of me. At the end of the ward was a private single room with a guy of a similar age. He was constantly on the phone, with people coming and going all day. I wondered who he was and what he was doing. It was clear he was running his business from his bed. I thought about my work and how much I needed to do. There was no way I could work from my bed. I was only just about holding it together doing virtually nothing.

The night was restless, frustrated again by tubes and pyjamas. The room was hot and stuffy but I felt cold and hollow, too tired to sleep. I catnapped, with my mind working hard to divert my attention from how low I felt.

Day three session three started badly, then went downhill. Just one session of etoposide and I could go. My head was heavy, my eyes bleary, my stomach flicking from tumble-dry to fast spin. It was probably only half an hour or so but seemed endless as wave after wave of nausea battered me into submission. Nurses bustled into action, ferrying sick bowls, wiping my face, being there, oh and pumping me full of anti-sickness drugs.

By lunchtime I had settled down but had not eaten any solids. There didn't seem much point, if they were going to bounce straight back up again. I had survived the etoposide and at last could go home. I longed to be at home, in my own environment curled up in my chair, in front of my telly, with my kitchen and my choice of food. Not that I could taste much of it.

"How are you feeling now, are you well enough to go home?"
"Much better thank you, nurse, I'm sure I'll rest better at home."
"All right then, I've just got one or two bits for you then you can go."

I looked up at Amanda and smiled. She smiled back but behind the smile I could see she was anxious. I needed her more than I would ever know, too absorbed in my own battle to begin to think what she was going through. The nurse returned with an armful of stuff.

"Right then, I've got two books for you, Eating well during treatment and Build yourself up. It's important that you get good nutrition to help you to recover."

"That's easier said than done, everything tastes bland, it's an effort to eat and even more of an effort to keep it down."

"He's mainly been eating scrambled eggs, or beans on toast, or soup," Amanda added.

"That's good, try to eat little and often, give your body a chance to absorb the food rather than a big meal which will tire you out. Remember you use energy to digest food so just pace yourself and you will feel better more quickly. Take care and we'll see you back in three weeks."

The next week or so was really hard work. I felt constantly cold, wrapped up in layers of T-shirts, jumpers and dressing gowns, my skin had a ghostly pallor, my face was drawn. My mouth was raw with ulcers and my teeth ached. I had no energy; the simplest of tasks drained me. The journey up or down stairs was an epic event, taking one step at a time. I was 30 going on 300. The shuffle from chair to kitchen had to be really worth my while. A hot-water bottle and a bowl were my constant companions. My mind kept going back to the nurse's advice. Keep eating little and often, keep drinking water to stay hydrated. It was hard to tell how much was getting through but I knew it would feel a lot worse retching on an empty stomach.

I was now being sick every other hour to the point where I just knelt by the loo, too tired to move, just waiting to retch again and again with nothing more to give. Amanda would pick me up, wipe my face with a warm flannel, the heat felt so good, and put me back to bed.

At times I barely knew where I was, my mind and body on autopilot. Round three was a decisive win for chemo. At night I lay awake telling myself I could get through this. Just deal with each day, each hour, each minute at a time. Concentrating on the good times ahead - we had a wedding to plan, a future together, a life to live.

Into week two and the sickness eased off. I felt I could eat more and became more confident that it would stay down. Still very weak, I could now climb the stairs in one motion go rather than stopping at each step. I began to sleep through the night and so it was, slowly day by day, I was getting back to some normality.

"Mark . . . The wig man's here."

"Morning, Mr Compton. I'm John Clarke from the NHS wig service. How are you today?"

In the doorway stood a smiling, cheerful chap with a smart suit and a large suitcase, much like a travelling salesman. By now, I was quite used to my bald head look and, to be fair, didn't really need a wig, but John was a breath of fresh air after a week when it would have been easier to give up than to keep on fighting.

"Could be better," I smiled. "Cup of tea?"
"That would be lovely, milk one sugar, please."

Amanda and I were transported to a faraway world of theatre as John opened up his box of hairpieces. This was dressing-up time and we were five years old again. Trying on wig after wig, posing in the mirror, falling about laughing, tears of joy as we took it in turns to make fools of ourselves.

The fashion of the time was for short hair, whereas John's collection was mostly stuck in the Seventies with Ziggy Stardust specials or Kevin Kegan perms on offer, with names such as Tarzan or Beast.

"We can cut the style to suit and they are fully washable."
"Do you feed it a saucer of milk?"

John was trying but he didn't have much to work with.

"Sorry, only kidding. Do you have anything fairly normal in brown?"

"Just the 'Paul McCartney', but after we trim it a bit you'll never know it's not real."

"Done. Sold to the man with the bald head."

The wig duly arrived a week later and after a couple of outings to show family and friends, it was resigned to a drawer never to be seen again.

By week three I was feeling a lot better, but still only 50 per cent of normal. I had managed a few short days at work but was finding the going tough. I didn't have the concentration I needed, but still preferred to be at work than at home. At least there I felt as though I was doing something positive, even if in truth I was doing very little.

The 2nd of March and we packed our bags for round four. I'd been dreading this day for some time. Still suffering the effects of round three, chemo was definitely on top and I had no appetite to get back in the ring for another pummelling. On the other hand this was the last round and after this I would be cured and the cancer gone. Was it worth it? Damn right it was worth it!

"Hello Mark, welcome back, your bed's ready. I just need to check you over first. OK?"

I thought back to my first session, the confident cocky young man announcing his arrival. How he differed from this quiet bloke who the nurses knew by name, an old hand at this game. Christmas was a world away.

"Morning nurse, this is a regular home from home but I shan't be sorry when it's over."

"You're doing very well, don't worry. Any problems over the last three weeks?"

"Just feeling really tired, constantly being sick, I've a couple of ulcers that won't go away. But otherwise better now, just jaded."

"OK. Let's take a look at your mouth. Mmm, have you been using the mouthwash and the soft toothbrush?"

"Yes, twice daily."

"OK. Well, let's try a stronger mouthwash. That should help you."

Amanda and I made our way on to the ward. This time my bed was in the top right hand corner. I thought back to session two, this was the bed Mary's sister-in-law had occupied. Don't be daft! I hurriedly thought of something else, not wanting to dwell on other patients less fortunate. It struck me that as the sessions went past I had moved further up the ward. Was this coincidence or was it a thought-out plan to move the worst patients further in so as not to upset the newcomers?

"Are you going to be OK?"

"Yep, I'm fine, I'm just keen to get this over and done with."

"Me too. I love you."

Amanda's eyes were welling up.

"I love you too, besides I've got Basil here to watch over me. Come back with food."

Nurse plumbed me in and after a dose of pre-hydration, cisplatin kicked off round four.

My body was tired and my senses dulled by the previous three rounds but still the smell of hospital was still all purveying. As I settled in and adjusted to my surroundings, the triggers inside me were already cocked and within the hour I was sick. As lunchtime came and dinner was served, I could feel the trolley take a grip of me. As a child I used to hate sponge puddings, the mere smell used to make me feel ill, so now it was with the food trolley, only now I really was ill and I really was being sick.

By the end of day one, I was back on the rollercoaster of chemo, with waves of nausea, cramps, sweating and feeling weary and irritable. I was not physically as bad as I had been in session three but now my mind was also weak. At night I lay half awake, thinking of the full enormity of what was happening to me.

Until now I had been mentally strong, always putting on a brave face, smiling at people when they looked at me saying, "Goodness you're brave," hardly bringing themselves to say the word cancer. I'm not brave. I didn't ask for cancer. I didn't have a choice in this. One day you're fine, the next you've got cancer. You just deal with it. Only now, here in a lonely hospital bed, late at night on round four of chemo, I wasn't dealing with it.

I was scared. I'd seen people die on this ward. They were old and weak and I am young and strong. I don't feel strong. I thought back to the young man I saw on my first session, he was young and strong, he looked in a worse state than I felt now. What happened to him? Did he make it? Has he recovered?

I prayed, I prayed to God that I would make it through this. I had spent all my energy keeping my mind and soul together whilst my body went through hell, now I needed more. In my mind's eye I visualised putting my hand in the hand of God. I felt Him grip firmly and a warm flow of energy pass down through my arm. I looked into His eyes and felt calm. In a blink the image was gone, but I felt stronger, I knew I could get through this.

Day two, session four; not long to go now, let's just get through the day and tomorrow I can go home. I was still feeling groggy but decided that I needed to take my mind off things. So drippy and I set off on the long walk to the common room in search of jigsaws and Connect Four.

"Hi, I'm Mark, fancy a game?"

"Why not? I'm Ray."

"Is this your first time Ray?"

"Yes, I'm not too sure what to expect. It all seems a bit daunting. How about you?"

"This is session four of four. I should be out of here for good tomorrow, touch wood."

Ray was older than me, we talked and played Connect Four and, in that time-honoured tradition, I passed on to him, just as Paul had to me, all the tricks of the trade. I reassured him that there were always better times ahead. How to check the flow of the drugs, to make sure he drank enough water. To say yes to the anti-sickness drugs, to take care of his mouth. To keep a warm flannel to hand. Not to overdo it, to rest at all times, to stay mentally active and, most important of all, to keep a positive attitude.

"How do you stay positive when you see all these patients around you?"

"Ray, it's simple. Just imagine yourself in a better place. It's easy. I've been reading a book called One by Richard Bach. You have it, maybe it can inspire you."

The day went quickly and that night I slept a lot better, the nausea was still there but not so aggressive. I still felt weak but tomorrow was my last day.

Day three, session four; if I thought it was getting easier I was wrong. With the morning came more waves of nausea, more being sick and more anti-sickness drugs. This time they didn't seem to have any effect and by lunchtime I felt pretty rough. I might have staged a comeback but chemo wasn't over yet.

After lunch, Amanda took me home. I was pleased to get away

from the hospital back to the sanctuary of home. The next week was to prove easier than after session three, but still the tiredness continued, the nausea continued. Slowly, gradually, it eased day by day.

Chapter Five

Amanda

We were back home, session two was over and we were trying to get back to everyday living again. Mark wasn't looking well. Of course, I didn't tell him that but he had certainly lost weight and didn't have as much colour in his face. He was clearly very tired and he slept whenever he wanted to. I'd often go up and look at him sleeping. The sickness had got worse, now he wasn't just feeling sick but he was being very sick. He wasn't eating much, so often he was just severely retching rather than throwing up anything.

At least asleep he was resting and calm and not feeling sick. Often at night he'd get up and I'd be woken by the sound of him being sick in the bathroom. One morning I woke to find him missing. He was in the bathroom, there was just about enough light in the room to see strands of his hair left behind on his pillow and on his side of the bed. I guessed this was the beginning of his hair loss.

I was downstairs watching television when I heard movement upstairs. He was up and coming downstairs in his dressing gown.

"I fancy something to eat."

"That's good," I said. "What do you fancy?"

"Not sure, something tasty but easy to eat."

I went into the kitchen and called back into the lounge with a selection of options.

"Oh, I don't know." There was a tone of irritability and impatience in his voice. I put both hands on the kitchen counter and counted to 10. Don't rise to it or get cross, I told myself. He's tired and I need to be patient.

"How about some scrambled eggs?"
Mark popped his head round the kitchen door and said: "Fine, that sounds good."
I smiled and he went off to freshen up with a shower while I was preparing his food.

I was just at that crucial point; scrambled eggs nearly done to perfection, toast in, when I was summoned.

"Amanda, come up here a minute can you?"

"I'm cooking. What is it?"

"Please, just come up."

I turned things off and quickly marched upstairs to the bathroom. I found Mark standing there, naked, holding his hands out –which were both covered in hairs.

"Oh my God," I said. He was laughing, fortunately, and I felt myself laughing too. There were clumps of hair in and on the side of the bath. This was it, this was another side-effect of this horrible treatment. As he combed his hair more and more came out until there were just a couple of tufts either side of his head.

"I'm sorry, I said, you can't look like that, it looks ridiculous."
So I picked up his clippers and as he sat on the side of the bath I ran them over his head. He stood up and looked in the mirror and we both smiled.

Losing hair for a man I guess is not as traumatic as for a woman but nonetheless it was a shock, especially as it all came out so quickly. He was lucky he had a nice-shaped head and we were advised that he should keep it warm; not just to stay warm but apparently it would encourage hair re-growth once treatment was over.

As the next couple of weeks went by, the sickness eased. Mark was still very tired but at least he could eat proper meals now and maybe regain some strength. We went over to visit my mother and, of course, Mark walking through the door bald headed was a real shock but people soon got used to it, as we did.

We had started to attend church on Sundays. We had already been to see the Reverend Charles Taylor about marrying us the following August. He was a great support to us during Mark's illness and Mark's name was always read out during the Sunday service for the congregation to pray for, which was very touching. I had never been particularly religious but I guess, like anyone during times of worry and uncertainty, you like to think there is someone out there with a guiding hand who might help during these times and answer your prayers.

Session three for chemotherapy was beckoning and I was worried this time that it would be an absolute beast. Could he take any more sickness? He was drained by it all, both physically and mentally and all I could do was to be there for him.

The nurses commented on his new no-hair look. I guess they were used to all this, but I think Mark still felt self-conscious about it when seeing people he'd met before. As we were on the subject they offered the services of the NHS wig department! Would he like to see someone? It's not something either of us had considered. I think maybe some women find a wig is essential but it is easier for a man to be bald. It was a free service, so we decided to accept.

Mark ran through how he'd been feeling since his last session. Pretty awful was the answer; very tired, very sick, mouth ulcers, feeling cold sometimes or feeling hot. Basically the whole body is buggered up and much as you want to keep going it becomes increasingly difficult.

Mark was shown to his bed, mid ward this time and no familiar faces around. I saw him into bed and then left for work. I visited as normal and took food. He'd still not been able to stomach anything provided by those trolleys apart from the odd cup of tea or pot of jelly. This session had been hard. He'd been very sick and I was anxious to get him home in the warm and in his own bed where he'd feel much better, I was sure.

It was the weekend, and we could have some time together. He wanted to be indoors most of the time in the warm. I sat in the bathroom with him, while he had a bath, with my cup of tea and we just chatted. I remember thinking how thin he looked. He now had no hair on his body at all which didn't help.

I remember thinking, is he disappearing in front of my eyes? Will he recover and feel better? Will we get to walk down the aisle in August? If we were to, it seemed that we had a long way to go. Mark's parents came over to visit and his dad got him out on a short walk around the block. He was all wrapped up with his cap on - you couldn't tell which one of them was the old man. When he returned he fell into the chair exhausted.

The sickness was becoming more frequent. He often just sat on the bathroom floor waiting for the next wave of nausea to come over him. There was little I could do except to be there with a cold flannel and make the bed comfortable when he felt able to get back to the bedroom and crawl into it. I wanted him to sleep, at least then he was resting, resting from being sick, resting from thinking about what he was going through.

The next couple of weeks became easier, the sickness wore off as it always did around this time and he was eating again and it was staying down! It was during this time that our friendly NHS wig man came calling. We were looking forward to this only because we knew it would give us a jolly good laugh.

He arrived with a case and began to take out its contents of hairpieces and wigs in various shapes, sizes and colours. So we chose one and were told it would be sent in the post a week or so later. We couldn't wait! When it arrived Mark tried it on and we laughed again. It had major entertainment value showing it off to family and friends but it remained in its box after that.

Early March was looming and we were soon off for round four of chemo. Mark's energy was flagging again but this was the final stretch, so at least once he was home this time we could say goodbye to "drippy" and get on with our lives. Nurses and doctors were on first name terms now and we always got a warm welcome when we pitched up for another session.

I left him to a day I knew wasn't going to be a barrel of laughs and made my way to work. There were colds going round the office and I had to be careful not to catch one, as if Mark got a cold now it would be awful for him.

His immune system was shot to pieces and he'd not cope with it well. I found the moaning and groaning of people at work with headaches and colds very annoying. It was just a cold! Seeing what Mark was going through really put things into perspective and having a cold was extremely trivial compared to what he was having to suffer. At times I felt like telling them so.

My two bosses, Paul and Chris, had been marvellous, very supportive, always letting me go when I needed to. It's very difficult trying to convey to others what it's like going through a serious illness. It wasn't happening to me but I was so close to it I felt as though it was at times. I remember Mark's friend, Ann, phoning to see how things were going, asking how he was and how the chemo was going, and then she said: ". . . and just as important, how are you?"

How was I? That was a question indeed. I'd just kind of been trundling along on autopilot to be honest and hadn't really stopped to think how I was. But it was nice to be asked.

People used to ask how on earth were we coping. Mark always used to say, "what choice do I have?" And indeed we didn't! This was with us and we had no choice but to get on with it and fight it. I was always incredibly proud of and amazed by how well Mark was coping. If the tables were turned and it had been me going through all that, I think I would have felt extremely sorry for myself and wanted to give up, but he never did.

I got home from work one day and Mark said: "I cried today." I hugged him and said I wasn't surprised. I'm sure I would have cried most days if I had been through all this. There were bound to be low points and he mustn't feel bad or be afraid of showing his emotions.

Day three of session four and I was on my way to collect Mark. I wasn't ready for the sight that greeted me. Yes he was ready, yes he was dressed but to my mind in no fit state to make the journey home. He was sitting cross-legged on his bed with a sick bowl in front of him and he was being sick. He was hot, looked extremely groggy and was being sick continually. The nurses were there and helping as best they could.

I busied myself putting the things from his locker into his bag so that as soon as he felt able to move we could be off home. He swung his legs round to dangle over the side of the bed and gingerly stood up, feeling a little lightheaded. I told him there was no rush and to take his time. I carried his bag and the nurse gave us a few of the lovely grey cardboard sick bowls for the journey!

I left Mark to sit in the reception area of the hospital while I brought the car round for him. I tried to drive as smoothly as possible but every bump, every pothole I could tell was an ordeal for him. At last we were driving into our Close and the safety of home. We were home, chemotherapy over, thank goodness. Mark took to his bed, exhausted from being sick and I left him to sleep.

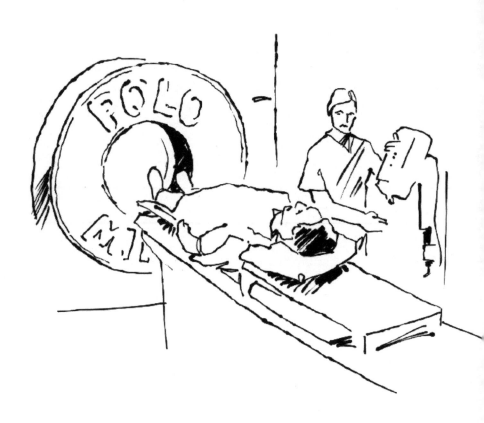

Chapter Six

Mark

Home at last, with chemo behind us we could start to think more about getting on with life. Dr Mead was confident that chemo should kill off the remaining specks and that would be the end of it. That was good enough for me.

For the next 10 days after round four I was still very weak, sickness came in waves, but it was nowhere near as intense as after round three. With a new sense of determination I strived to feel better and better each day.

Slowly I returned to work, at first just doing short days and then building day on day. The guys at work had been very supportive in a "don't mention the war" style, and mostly treated me with kid gloves, which suited me just fine. I managed to put away a couple of deals probably with more help than I care to recall but as every recruiter will tell you making a deal gives you a real buzz and that was the sort of motivation I needed right now.

Whether it was the knowledge that I would not have to do this again, I'm not sure, but each minute, each hour, each day I could feel myself climbing out of the volcano of chemotherapy. Behind me was the pit of nausea, of constant sickness and weakness, and ahead of me were clear blue skies and meadows.

"We've got an appointment with Charles the vicar this afternoon. Are you up to it?"

Putting yourself through chemotherapy is an extreme but effective way of avoiding the runaway train that is planning a wedding, but with chemo over I really had no excuses. Our wedding was in the diary for August 6th a mere five months away.

"That's fine, what do we need to talk about?"

Like many other couples in England, we had met, fallen in love, proposed, and then become regular church goers. Charles was an excellent vicar, destined for higher office, who had just the right level of common sense and compassion mixed in with a healthy understanding of the real world. He had followed our story right from the start and my name had been a regular on the please-pray-for list each week. After my last session of chemo, I was beginning to believe they could be right.

The vicarage was a true gothic masterpiece with an imposing façade and large studded wooden doors.

"Welcome, welcome, come on in, through to the study."
Charles's study was befitting a busy vicar, with piles of books and papers, notes about garden fetes, next week's sermon, last week's sermon. Through all this organised chaos, Charles knew where everything was. It was in this office that Amanda and I had first sat down with Charles and explained our past, talked through our beliefs and he had agreed to marry us in the pretty church of North Stoneham.

"Mark, how are you? How are you feeling now that you've finished your treatment?"

"Relieved mostly, glad it's all over, I certainly wouldn't want to do that again. I'm still recovering, getting back my appetite and my strength but mostly just happy it's all over."

"… and Amanda, more importantly, how are you coping?"

"I'm glad he's home, it's been quite a stressful time, juggling work, visiting him, feeding him, worrying about him. I think I could do with a holiday just to recharge the batteries, which is partly why we are here today. Mark's been very ill, he, we, have both been through a lot over the last three months and I'm not sure we will be ready in time for an August wedding."

Amanda was right, weddings can be stressful enough in their own right and right now Amanda and I were both emotionally drained.

"Can we move the wedding back a few months? I think we need space to draw breath and recover a bit. I want to enjoy the day with Mark and make it a celebration. I've got him this far, I'm not letting him go now."

Charles smiled at Amanda with a compassionate face.
"You know, sometimes people don't realise how much of a toll illness can have on people. They get so swept up in events that they don't fully absorb what it's doing to them, both physically and spiritually. I think you both are a wonderful couple and you are right to give yourselves some space, reflect on recent events, and then to enjoy and take in the full meaning of your wedding and what that means to you both… So, where's my diary?"

Several minutes later after much shuffling of papers, a diary was found. Charles was keen to take the ceremony personally, which meant a couple of phone calls to rearrange other events and then finally we settled on October 1st.

As Amanda drove us home from the vicarage, there was a palpable sense of relief. We had both been through the wringer, and now we had a sensible date to focus on and a wedding to plan; but, for now, just switching off and relaxing, thinking of absolutely nothing was a rare and precious moment.

"Take a seat in waiting area B."

This was my third visit to the CT scanner so, as an old hand, I knew where to place my x-ray pack, and duly took a seat. I had come prepared in easy-to-change clothes and had a sports bag to put my stuff in.

The waiting area was like a cross between a school staff room, a locker room and a hospital. To one side there were changing cubicles with those never-quite-fitting curtains, designed for very slim small people. To the other was an arrangement of chairs around a coffee table with pin boards on the walls, both scattered with out-of-date posters and pamphlets. Nurses came and went, striding with purpose and never stopping long enough to chat. Elderly and infirm patients were wheeled in and then wheeled away again. I was never sure if they were being x-rayed or it was just a convenient place to park them while they shuffled beds.

"Mark Compton."
"Yes, that's me."
"Orange or blackcurrant?"
"Does it make a difference?"
"Well, we like to think so."
"Orange then, please."
"OK, if you could get changed into a gown I'll bring out your drink. Drink this slowly over the next hour and save a bit for when you go through."

The orange tasted pretty much like the blackcurrant, which is to say metallic; 50 minutes later, full of fluid, I was flat on my back entering the giant polo.

"Breathe in . . . And breathe away . . ."

At my first scan, this bit had seemed like hard work, now after four rounds of chemo, my breathing was much more shallow and I was much more relaxed about the whole thing.
"OK, you're done."

Wow, that was painless. Straight to the loo to lose a litre of liquid tin.

I still didn't like hospitals. This was two weeks now since the end of chemo, and although still jaded and feeling like an old man, my strength and faculties were coming back. Just one more session with Ben to confirm this was over and we could all go back to normality.

"Hello, hello, how are you? How was chemo? We've had another five cases since I last saw you, fascinating." Dr Mead was as ever enthusiastic about his work. His rapid-fire speech brimmed with energy.

"Morning, Dr Mead, good to see you again. I'm all right, still very tired and just weary really, but I feel as though I'm getting brighter by the day."
"Good, good."
"I'm just glad chemo is over. I don't want to go through all that again."

"Right, let's have you up on the bed, take a look at you."
Trolleys down, lying back on the bed, Dr Mead set about checking my bits and prodding me in the stomach.
"Does that hurt?"
My stomach had taken a pounding coming through chemo and had perfected a great party piece impersonating a tumble dryer - Dr Mead's prodding wasn't doing me any favours.

"It's a bit sore still, but no sharp pain."

"OK, get dressed and come back and sit down."

I sorted myself out and sat back down next to Amanda, waiting for Dr Mead to pronounce the all clear.

"We've had a look at your scan, and the grey areas that were there before are still there. If anything they may be a little bit bigger. So, where we would have expected the chemotherapy to reduce these areas, that hasn't happened, I'm afraid. I'm still confident these are just teratoma differentia, but what this means is that we need to whip them out."

So that's not an all clear then. Ben was still talking, but my mind was shouting louder and louder and I still wasn't hearing the words.

"Sorry, so are you saying that the chemo hasn't changed anything?"

"That's right. It was still the right thing to do. We have to be sure we've got it, nipped it in the bud, and we don't like to perform surgery unless we have to."

"So, I'm still not sure I understand. Is this malignant? Is it still spreading?"

The word cancer was still not being used by either party. Amanda, sitting by my side, was quiet and pensive - whole pound coins were dropping in her mind while I was still having trouble with the pennies.

"No, no, there is no sign of any additional spreading but the grey areas we can see haven't shrunk and they are consistent with a right testis teratoma so, to be on the safe side, we will just whip them out. That way we can be certain of what we are dealing with."

My mind had been working overtime to get me through chemo

and now it was tired, and I really wasn't getting what Ben was saying to me.

"So the chemo has had no effect?"

"Well it has had an effect, it just hasn't been as effective as we would have hoped for. This is perfectly normal, certainly worthwhile. No case is ever the same, so we have to try all the options. Now we'll give you some time to recover from your chemotherapy and then have you back in to whip these bits out."

"No more chemo?"

"No."

"But back in hospital?"

"Yes."

"When?"

"A couple of weeks . . . probably the first week in April."

This was a struggle. Why hadn't the chemo just zapped the bad guys? What does he mean, just whip them out? The last time they "just whipped one out" I lost a bollock! I thought he said they don't like to perform operations unless they are absolutely necessary.

"What are you going to do?"

"Well, the suspect areas are near the base of your spine, so what we will do is go in through your tummy, whip them out and put you back together again. You'll be in hospital for a good week and then need complete rest for a further two to three weeks."

"Surgery?"

"Yes, Mr Smart will be the surgeon. He performed your orchidectomy, I can arrange for him to have a talk with you if you like."

"Surgery? In two weeks?"

"Yes, it's for the best."

"Near the base of my spine?"

"It's all perfectly normal, just routine. Mr Smart is a very good surgeon, nothing to worry about, less than five per cent ever have any complications; you are in very good hands."

Just what part of cutting someone open, fishing around in their guts, cutting out bits and then sewing them back up is considered NORMAL? I'd slipped into movie mode, this wasn't happening to me. This wasn't real. This was just some scene in a movie with a happy-ever-after ending. It did have a happy-ever-after ending, didn't it? And still no Felicity Kendal!

Amanda was chipping in with her own set of questions but I wasn't fully paying attention, my mind was in crisis, with alarm bells ringing and all hands to the pumps to get me out of there.

I hadn't noticed but Amanda and I were holding hands united in our efforts to absorb this body blow. We left Ben's surgery and made our way down to the cafeteria. Beans on toast and builders' tea did little to lighten the mood. When does this all end? Just as you think you've got it licked, someone writes another chapter. So what do you do? What can you do? You just dig deep and steel yourself for the next round.

Chapter Six

Amanda

Over the next couple of weeks Mark tried to regain more strength. I think mentally, knowing chemo was over motivated him to get stronger and try to get back to a normal life.

It was now early March; I've always loved this time of year as spring arrives, the air is fresher and the evenings lighter. I hated winter and it seemed more significant this year, coming out from a darkness that had certainly been more than just the winter.

But there was always a tinge of sadness for me at this time of year. It was this time of year that my Dad had been taken from us so suddenly with a heart attack. I miss him still, of course, although it does get easier as the years go by. Sadness is replaced by nice memories and thoughts of what he'd be like now. But thoughts of my wedding coming up later in the year, and wishing he was here made it very hard for me.

Mark's strength wasn't returning quickly, and I did wonder if the August date we had set for the wedding was too soon. We had been through a lot and I really wanted this to be a special day that we could both enjoy to the full. For that he'd need to be fully fit.

I was nervous about bringing the subject up with Mark because I didn't want to disappoint him, but I had talked to Mum about it and she too thought it was a good idea. We'd done next to nothing about arrangements for the wedding and there was so much to do. So I spoke to Mark about it and at first he seemed reluctant. "I'll be fine . . . it's a way off yet," was his response. However, in the end he did see sense and agreed we'd go and talk to the vicar to see if he could offer us another date.

We drew up outside the vicarage one dark wet evening; Charles greeted us at the door.

"Come in, come in," he said, waving his hand ushering us through to his office. We took our seats and Charles sat on his rather old looking leather studded wing chair.

He asked how we'd both been and Mark ran through what had been rather a tough time for us both. Charles had been with us from the start of all this and had been a great support; reading Mark's name out in church on Sundays for prayers along with others who were poorly or just needed God's help.

We had tried to go along to church regularly since signing up to get married and it soon became apparent that we weren't just going through the motions as many engaged couples do leading up to their wedding. I felt we were there for a purpose now; OK that might be a selfish thing to think but I did find it a comfort. If there was ever a time we needed help, this was it.

Charles was very sympathetic when we brought up the subject of shifting the date a few months. He understood what we'd been through and agreed we needed time to adjust and get things back to normal again. Weddings are stressful enough and we needed some breathing space and, I guess, just to be together for a bit. So, October 1st was agreed and we drove home feeling somewhat relieved we'd bought ourselves a bit of time.

The next appointment for Mark's CT scan was quickly upon us and so off we went back to the South Hants. Out came the large plastic jug of fruit juice... mmm, if only!

Mark changed into his fetching gown once again and we waited in the lounge area for him to do his drinking. There was always quite a bit of bustle going on; nurses and doctors coming and going, outpatients, people in beds, people in wheelchairs, all waiting their turn to go into that machine. This was all becoming routine for Mark by now. As I sat in the waiting room he went in to be done. The large doors closed behind him and the red light came on as the large magnetic scanner went into action. Having worked in television news this always reminded me of the "on air" light outside the studios but there was a crew of a different kind in this room and what would be the news they delivered? Good, I hoped.

The next day we were back in front of Dr Mead for the results. Ben was his usual blustery self, shaking us by the hand as we took a seat.

"So how are things?" he said with a beaming smile, looking first at Mark then at me.

"Not too bad," Mark replied. "Getting better each day, regaining some strength again and able to taste real food again, which is nice."

Ben took Mark into the side examination room and I sat and waited. Mark's medical file was open in front of me, upside down. I was trying to see what it said. It was full of scribbled notes and very suspect-looking drawings, numbers and medical terminology. Even if I could read upside down it probably wouldn't mean anything. They returned from the examination room and Ben carried on talking.

"OK, the dark areas at the base of your spine are still visible on this latest scan, I'm afraid. It seems the chemotherapy hasn't reduced them at all."

This was not the news I was expecting to hear. I frowned and felt myself getting a little angry.

"What do you mean the chemotherapy hasn't worked? What, not at all?"

"No I'm afraid not."

"So what was the point of all that then?"

I was finding it very difficult to understand why Mark had been put through four sessions of gruelling chemotherapy for nothing. How could this be? Has he any idea what we've been through? Well I guess he does - he sees it all the time. But to actually live so closely to someone going through something so awful - I was annoyed and angry that we had been put through the wringer, for what, for nothing?

"It's right to try chemo first rather than just going in with major surgery, but in this case we are going to have to remove them with an operation."

I looked at Mark; he was clearly not happy either and felt his world had probably just collapsed. We had just started to feel more positive about things and look ahead to the wedding and getting on with life. This came was a major blow.

Ben said he'd give Mark a bit more time to get over his tiredness but we were looking at a date in early April for the surgery. I was so glad now that we'd postponed the wedding. With major surgery to come there was no way Mark would be ready. Ben talked through more of what the surgery would entail but I was switching off, he clearly had to have it and that was that.

We left Ben's office and went down to the canteen to have some tea and toast, a place we had often retreated to after seeing Ben. It was very much needed. I was feeling very sorry for Mark - he understandably didn't like hospitals and the thought of going back in there again with pyjamas and wash bag so soon, just didn't seem fair and this time he'd be in for longer.

So off we were again - phone calls and visits to relatives to update them on the next stage. Everyone was sympathetic and offered to help but really nice as they were, there was little anyone could do. Mark's family were not the best in these circumstances - yes they were keen to hear what was happening, but as far as rallying round and coming down to visit they weren't as forthcoming as I felt they should have been.

So I kind of felt I was pretty much flying solo. My Florence Nightingale hat would come out again and with the help of my mum, who was an absolute stalwart, we'd cope with what was to come.

Chapter Seven

Mark

"Have you got everything?"

"Yes, I think so. Where's Basil?"

"I don't know. Where did you leave him?"

"If I knew that I wouldn't be asking would I!"

"There he is on top of the wardrobe. Honestly, Mark you can't see things in front of your face sometimes."

Well it's easy to mislay an eight-inch reindeer when your mind's on other things. Packing for hospital was a task I had thought I wouldn't need to do for a while, but here I was with freshly laundered pyjamas, dressing gown, bizarre shoe-like things called slippers, a toothbrush (soft) and, finally, a cuddly toy.

"I'll have to drop you at the entrance, I'm not sure I'll find a parking space."

"OK. I'll wait for you in the lobby."

Southampton General was a very different kettle of fish from the Royal South Hants. I had been to the General before for the orchidectomy. It was a much larger hospital with floor after floor, corridor after corridor all looking much the same. You could see how easy it would be to lose things here. People often did, mostly body parts. Last time I came here I lost a testicle.

Amanda parked and we made our way up to men's surgical on the fifth floor.

"Morning, I'm Mark Compton, I was asked to report here."

"Hello Mark, be with you in just a minute. Ah yes, we have a bed ready for you. I'll take you down there shortly, if you could just fill out this form."

With the preliminaries over, nurse led me to the ward.

"Toilets and washrooms are over there, and your bed is the end one next to the window. All right now, you're booked in for surgery tomorrow, if you wish you can have a light lunch but no more food after that. Doctor will be round to explain what they are going to do later on. I'll leave you to settle in."

The view from my bed was fantastic. I could see for miles across Southampton. It was fascinating and kept me occupied for hours. Amanda checked I was all right and left to go back to work. As she walked away, I sat on the edge of my bed and looked around the ward, then out of the window. Oh, what I would give to be free, to be outside, with the wind in my hair - hair, what hair? And not cooped up in hospital again.

It was five weeks now since my last session of chemo and probably three weeks since I had been sick. I had made a steady recovery and now the doctors deemed I was strong enough to undergo surgery. They certainly didn't want to waste time. There was no chance of having a week or two in the sun before they cut me open.

I had been anxious that morning, anticipating the events to come, so had not had much breakfast and was looking forward to a bite to eat. I could hear the bustle of dinner ladies working their way down the corridor; good they'd be here soon.

"Hello luv, you're new, are you allowed lunch?"
"Yes please, what have you got?"

"Shepherd's pie and strawberry jelly."
"That I'll be fine, with a cup of tea to wash it down."

As the dinner ladies moved on along the wards, I looked down at my shepherd's pie; the smell of hospital food, of the crockery and the trays infiltrated my head. It was a smell I recognised all too well. Toilets straight ahead! My stomach had gone into full spin. Not half an hour on the ward, still in civvies, five weeks after chemo I was being sick. I stood in the loos, looking at my face in the mirror. All of the colour had drained from my face, and my mind went back to the days of chemo and Hamilton Fairley. I can't let this get the better of me. This is mad; it's all in the mind . . . well, mostly down the toilet with some on my collar. Come on Mark. You can do this.

Back out on the ward, I looked again at my shepherd's pie and decided discretion was the better part of valour. At least there was strawberry jelly. I tipped the jelly out on to the plate and just watched it wobble. You can't help but smile at wobbly jelly.

"Mark isn't it? I'm the doctor responsible for you. How are you settling in?"
"Hello, yes, not so great, doctor. I think I'm suffering the after effects of chemo, the smell of the food trolley just made me feel sick. I was sick earlier when it came round but feel more settled now."
"Are you nervous about your surgery tomorrow?"
"Not really nervous. I tend to simply switch off and not think too much about the consequences. I trust you guys know what you're doing. But I would like to know what it is you are actually going to do."

"OK. Mr Smart is the surgeon who will be performing the operation. He's a very good surgeon; you'll meet him tomorrow.
Now, you know that you have secondary tumours that are essentially at the base of your spine. These have to be removed but we have to be careful not to upset any other parts of your body as

we do this. So we are going to perform a laparotomy. This means we will make an incision through your stomach, essentially move your other organs out of the way to get to the part we need to get to. Remove the offending articles, put everything back in place, sew you up and then we're done."

"You make that sound so simple. Will it hurt?"
"No, we will give you a pre-med about an hour before surgery then we hand you over to the anaesthetist who will knock you out. You won't feel a thing. However, this is major surgery and we have to cut through the stomach wall. This means that recovery will take three to four weeks and you will not be able to lift heavy objects or strain the stomach muscles for quite some time. But otherwise you will be fine."

"How long will the surgery take?"
"About two to three hours. OK?"
"OK."
"Good. No more solids before surgery. You can drink water and have a cup of tea for breakfast but that's it. I'll see you tomorrow."

With the doctor gone, I tried to get some rest. Now I just wanted to get on with it. That night I slept very well, all things considered.

"Mr Compton, I'm Smart. I'll be performing your surgery today. How are you feeling this morning, any complaints?"

Mr Smart was a dapper chap with a sharp blazer and tie, a moustache and the mannerisms of an RAF officer. I half expected him to say "chocks away" but luckily there were no chocs in sight, just some grapes in a bowl.

"Good morning, sir. No complaints, just raring to get up there and give the Bosh a good hiding, what!" Well, I wanted to say that.

"Good morning, Mr Smart. No, I'm fine, just keen to get on with this really, not so keen on the sitting-around-waiting bit."

"Good, that's the spirit. Well, I'll see you later."

I, on the other hand, won't see a thing.

The morning passed by fairly quickly as various doctors and nurses came and went. Checking my weight, height, what drugs I have had, any other medications, next of kin, and so on. Eileen, Amanda's mother came to see me, armed with chocolates and magazines.

I never really knew what to say to Eileen, and by now the pre-med was beginning to take effect making me drowsy. I think we talked about the view but it could have been the life and times of Tom Jones for all I knew but then I guess it's not unusual to have these sorts of conversation with mothers-in-law.

"Trolley for Mark Compton."

Hospital porters are always happy souls, wheeling patients back and forth, and mine today were no exception.

"Where to today, sir? We've got a lovely tour of the docks, and then later on to the theatre."
I smiled back: "Is the show any good? I've heard some cutting reviews."
"You just lie back and enjoy the ride."

It's a strange feeling lying on a trolley being pushed through a hospital. I kept thinking of Police Academy and imagined a red flashing light on the front of the bed as we swung from corridor to lift and then out into theatre land.

"Just wait there a sec. I'll check where you need to go."

I did think of making a run for it but decided I wouldn't get far in an operating gown.

"Hello Mark, I'm your anaesthetist today. How are you feeling?"
"Just a bit drowsy but quite calm."
"Good. Can you confirm your date of birth for me?"
"1/12/62"

I thought back to the orchidectomy and the daft conversation we had had about worm charming - probably not worth bringing that one up again. The room was very bright, a bit like a dentist's surgery but instead of leaning back in a chair I was laid out on a trolley looking up at the bright light panels. The anaesthetist was gowned up, with a mask over his face, preparing some mysterious concoction.

"OK. Now I'm about to ask you to count backwards from 10 and when you come back round it will all be over. OK?"
Counting 10, 9...8...7....6.....5.............

The orange light was the inside of my eyelids. Flickers of noise, voices, like spinning the tuning dial on an old radio, louder then softer, clearer then fuzzier. A veil of eyelashes, shielding my view, images, blurry, moving about. As my consciousness kicked in, the images became sharper and the noises became clearer.

"Mark? Can you hear me? Mark? Just squeeze my hand."

Hand? Where's the control for hands? I could hear the request and now I could feel the hand. Give me a minute and there it is, squeeze.

Amanda, Eileen, Mum and Dad, assorted faces were sitting around the bed. I was back on the ward, feeling cocooned, not really aware of my surroundings, slowly regaining feeling as my arms and legs, fingers and toes checked in and reported for duty.

Over the next hour or so, I became more and more alert. Not really saying much, just lying there. I was wrapped in bandages all around my middle, with tubes in and out of my body. The bedclothes felt tight, holding me in. I couldn't move, didn't want to move, time had no significance right now.

I remained pretty much in a semi-conscious state for the next day and a half, plumbed into an IV drip, drifting in and out of sleep. When I was awake I was very drowsy and not totally with it. Visitors came and smiled and made small talk but I don't really remember too much. I'm told my blood pressure was dangerously low at one point and so a blood transfusion was called for.

"Mark? Are you awake? Mark?"
I opened my eyes but didn't speak. A nurse was at my side, holding my hand and tapping my arm.
"Can you hear me? All right, I'm just going to talk you through what we have done and what we need to do now to get you up and about. OK, firstly you'll still be feeling the effects of the anaesthetics; that's what's making you groggy. They will wear off over time. It's important for you to keep drinking, OK? You're on a drip but we need you to drink and start to get your systems back up and working, OK? Yes?"

I was still very groggy but nodded and smiled at the nurse.

"All right, are we going to drink some water?" Nurse held a cup of water up to my mouth; I began to sip, slowly at first. It tasted horrible. I coughed, my stomach fired off shots of pain.
"Ahh! Can I have Ribena instead?"
"I'll check but that should be OK."

The nurse went away and came back some time later with Ribena.
"I've got you some Ribena. Now are you going to drink this for me?"

Again I began to sip slowly. As I drank I began to feel sick again and just heavy around my stomach.

"OK, we'll pop an NG tube in which will help us get some food into you. We need you to start taking nutrients on board to build up your strength."

The next thing I knew two nurses were trying to push a tube up my nose, which was not going well! As a result of a much earlier cycling accident, the bit in the middle of my nose was bent to one side restricting the size of my nostril. The feel and smell of the tube as they tried to force it where there was no room to force, was intense.

I flailed my arms sending the tube and nurse off to one side. I was not a happy bunny. A third nurse was called as they came in for a second attempt. I don't care how ill I am or how much good it's going to do me, you are absolutely not shoving that up my nose! Still groggy, I repelled boarders for a second time. Reluctantly, the nurses agreed that a third attempt would cause me too much stress. Damn right they had caused me too much stress!

I still wasn't eating properly and really only sipping peppermint water, but knew that I needed to try to eat solids. But, literally after chemo and a laparotomy, I didn't have the stomach for it.

By now it was day four post op. Nurses came and went, the sound of dinner ladies chattering, then the faint distant voice of Mr Smart some way down the corridor.

As the dinner ladies came closer the odour of hospital food grew.

"Arrghh!" "Arrghh!" My stomach convulsed tugging at the surgeon's needlework. In one move I was sitting up clutching my stomach. The pain was right off the scale. An excruciatingly sharp pain in the pit of my stomach. The air turned blue as I screamed out a torrent of expletives.

Visitors scattered as nurses rushed to give aid.

"It's the smell of the food trolley, it makes him feel sick," Amanda protested.

"Get him in that room NOW!" Mr Smart had also sprung into action and instantly I was wheeled into a private room to the side of the ward. With the door shut and a hefty shot of painkillers, I began to calm down.

"God, that really hurt! Ow! Now I'm awake. Christ, I do NOT want to do that again!"

For the rest of the evening, I just lay still, concentrating on not moving my stomach. I couldn't have rolled over, even if I had wanted to.

The next morning I began to come to terms with the magnitude of the operation I had been through. My stomach was still sore and my whole body ached.

"Hi Mark. I'm Richard your post-op nurse for the next few days. You gave us all a bit of a scare yesterday. How are you feeling now?"

"Hi. Still groggy and generally battered. My stomach aches and I've got bandages and tubes everywhere. When can I go home?"

"Good, I can see you are more alert today. That's good. OK. Now you have had major surgery, so we need to give you time for the body to recover. You will be here for at least a week and then need to recuperate at home for at least two to three weeks. Is there someone at home who can look after you?"

"Amanda is at work during the day. I'm not sure."

"OK. We'll sort something out. Now, you have a number of tubes in you, the one on the side is a drain from the wound to release any excess fluids. The other is a catheter, which takes urine from your bladder, OK? So what we now need to do is to get your bodily functions working again, which means we need to get you eating."

"I'm not going anywhere near a food trolley. There's no way I'm going through that again!"

"All right, I'll get the nutritionist to come and talk to you, but in the meantime let's try you on easy foods. I've got some Fortisips, which are a concentrated nutrition drink. We'll start with those. If you need me just press the buzzer."

As Richard left the room, I began to take on board what he had said to me. Up to that point pretty much all my effort had been concentrated on just being, staying still and not making anything hurt. The slightest movement of my tummy still felt like continental plates shifting, with ripples of pain emanating from the epicentre.

I set about planning my escape; I really did not want to be in hospital any longer than I absolutely had to. I looked around the room and thought back to Mr Smart. Getting a private room was the best move of the whole campaign. I just knew that the open ward would have presented a whole bunch of distractions and smells; NO don't think of smells! My stomach began to turn at the mere thought of the dinner trolley. The volume knob was beginning to turn up as the pain became more intense.

"All right, Mark, easy does it. Just take a deep breath - and again. OK?"

A nurse had responded to the buzzer and with little more than a box of tissues and a calming voice had settled me back down. My breathing was heavy and my stomach sore but nothing like the pain I had felt the day before.

"Sorry, I just came over, felt sick and then frightened, I didn't want to move my stomach." I wasn't really making much sense.

"It's OK. You will have episodes like this, you did the right thing by pressing the buzzer, just rest now. Richard will check on you in a while."

Buzzer? I don't remember pressing a buzzer. Must rest.

The door opened and in trooped a brother, sister-in-law, two nieces and a nephew. They took up positions around the bed and just sat there, staring at me. I wondered why they were all here? What had brother told the children? "Uncle Mark's got cancer, we have to go and see him." What questions would the children ask? "Is he going to die?" An eternity passed before my brother spoke.

"We weren't sure how many visitors you were allowed but thought Sunday was a good day to come . . . You look well."

Sunday? I had totally lost track of days, I came in on Tuesday, was operated on on Wednesday.

"Mum said she thought you were up to visitors, we've brought you some grapes."

What happened to Thursday?

"We'll let you get some rest." With that, they all duly filed out leaving me to ponder over the missing days.

In the corner of the room was an en suite shower and loo. Taking up on Richard's instructions, I knew that before I could go home, I had firstly to get myself to the loo and secondly pee and poo.

The first major obstacle to this cunning plan was that I was still plumbed into a catheter and a drain. Solid food was still causing me problems and nausea, so I set about drinking Fortisips as quickly and as often as I could. My particular favourite was banana but, let's face it, I would have drunk pretty much any flavour at that moment. It became a game with Richard, constantly requesting more Fortisips and asking when he would remove the tubes. As more drink went in, more fluid came out and I began to build my strength. Richard was monitoring the output and finally agreed the flow was good enough and controlled enough to take out the pipework.

Until now I hadn't really thought about the tubes inside me or where they were. The first to come out was the drain from the wound, a fair-sized pipe coming out of my side. Richard eased the tube out. I didn't really feel a thing other than a slight sensation as the tube finally came out. Richard dressed the wound left behind by the hole where the drain had been and then turned his attention to the catheter. As the bandages and tapes came away, the obvious dawned on me.

"Bloody hell! How did you get that tube down there?"
"Well it's the best way to get to your bladder. It's really just like feeding in a straw." A whole new meaning to cocktails flashed through my mind.

As he eased the catheter out, I couldn't look. I scrambled through my mind trying to find an image or a thought to hold on to and not think about what was actually happening. Despite this, all I could feel was the sensation of the tube pulling through places where tubes shouldn't be; a short-lived but supremely weird ordeal. Pass me another Fortisips.

"Amanda, it's me, they have said I can go home today. Can you come and get me?"

"That's good news, are you sure you are ready?"
"I don't want to stay here any longer than I have to."
"OK, I'll be there as soon as I can."

Within half an hour I was packed and ready to go, sitting on my bed, waiting. Some three hours later, Amanda arrived and I said my goodbyes and very gingerly made my way to the car. I was cautiously grateful that this ordeal was over. I never wanted to go back to a hospital ever again, ever.

Basil

Chapter Eight

Mark

As much as I was eager to leave hospital, I was still in a very delicate state. My body was battered and bruised from the surgery and I had a 10-inch wound in my stomach where Mr Smart had gained entry. Having come off the back of chemotherapy, I was still very weak as well as sore. Any movement of my core was painful. I needed complete rest.

We had talked through the options of where I would recuperate and with Amanda needing to work, Eileen had stepped into the breach. It made sense as Eileen could keep an eye on me during the day but I was still a little anxious at the thought of staying with mother-in-law, in a relatively strange place.

"Your room's all ready. It's Amanda's old room so you should be fine in there. It's just across the hall from the bathroom, so not too far for you to go when you've got to go."

This is so embarrassing; being in a private room in hospital is one thing but the thought of needing to 'go' in the future mother-in-law's house when the sheer act of 'going' was a military manoeuvre was not something I wanted to think about. Right now I just wanted rest - to sleep for a week and wake up mended.

"Are you hungry? I can do you some chicken soup."
"That would be lovely, thank you. I really just want to rest."

The chicken soup tasted so delicious. I knew I needed to eat and was still nervous of solids. The soup was just right. Afterwards Amanda helped me into bed and I was asleep before my head hit the pillow.

After two weeks I was becoming more mobile, my head was clearing, thoughts of the wedding were now gathering pace and, as my strength improved, Amanda and Eileen were involving me more and more in all the things we needed to do. Up to this point, I had mostly been a passenger on this runaway train, but now it was good to get involved and take my mind away from illness and surgery.

I had proposed to Amanda in the previous summer, before any thoughts of cancer. We had met, moved in together and were getting on well. This one's for keeps.

"This is a lovely restaurant Mark."
"Yes, it is. I'm glad you like it, I chose it especially for you. Would you like to play a game of 'twist or stick'? It could be fun."
"Maybe. How does it work?" Amanda was not too sure.
"Well, I'd like to give you a gift but want it to be something you really want. So I suggest a gift and you can either 'stick' and I'll get you that gift or you can twist and I'll suggest another one. But you only get one gift."

"OK. This could be fun."
"All right, first shot." I handed Amanda an envelope from my jacket pocket. Inside was a card with the words 'a box of chocolates'.
"Mmm … twist."
"OK. Try this." A second envelope, inside a card: 'Would you like a ride in a hot air balloon?'
"Oooh, I would . . . but I'll twist."

A third envelope: inside, a picture of a Labrador puppy.
By now Amanda was smiling broadly, we had talked about getting a dog, as we both loved them.

"A dog? I'd love a dog, a puppy."
"Stick or twist?"
"Oooh, I don't know."
"Stick or twist?"
"Ohhh. Twist."
"Damm, I thought you'd go for the dog." I paused and drew breath.

I reached inside my jacket and pulled out another envelope.
Amanda opened the envelope, inside was a ring.

"Will you marry me?"

"Yes, yes, yes!"

The bulk of decisions had been made by now. The church was booked, bridesmaids selected. Mum was to make the bridesmaids' dresses and guest numbers agreed, with a proviso that the Compton family would not outnumber the sum of Amanda's family plus friends.

A traditional white wedding; followed by a wedding breakfast with an evening do to follow. With the change of date came a change of venue. The original choice had been Marwell zoo and I admit I had had visions of a bun fight at the zoo with all the animals joining in. Thankfully, changing the date now meant we could now go to the Potter's Heron, a much more befitting venue.

There was one large hole in Amanda's life, and not an easy one to fill. She had been very close to her father, and his early passing had hit her hard, as it had Eileen and Amanda's sisters too.

Ken and Eileen - very confusing as they had the same names as Amanda's parents - were lifelong friends of Amanda's parents and we were all pleased as punch when Ken agreed to give Amanda away.

"Which would you prefer? Photos or video?"

"Both. You can't have a wedding without a photographer and I think a video would be a real keepsake. Besides, the video will capture those 'off camera' moments. We should have both."

Amanda was quite into photography and video. With her background in TV, I was probably on a hiding to nothing.

"We don't need both, anyway photos will just sit in the drawer collecting dust. We have to save money somewhere, so if we have a video then I don't think we need a photographer."

"Don't worry about the money, it's covered. Besides I have a few contacts who can help."

Gary was the videographer who had been recommended. He was local and had done some good work and now we were on his doorstep.

"Hi, I'm Gary, come on through."

Gary was an ageing skinhead, with close-cropped hair and a wiry body with tight jeans and tattoos.

"It's all right, I'll dress up proper for the big day."

There was a happy levity in Gary's voice and, despite his appearance, I felt a healthy level of respect.

Gary led us down the garden path, literally, to his video studio in a large shed at the end of his garden. He showed us examples of his work and we agreed to hire him. As we chatted, Amanda opened up about our recent history and how I had just come through chemo and cancer. Gary looked at me again and I sensed a different energy.

"Oh, I thought the haircut was by choice."

I smiled, "Sadly not, but I quite like it this way."

A few things fell into place. Since chemo and losing my hair some people had acted differently around me. Often old ladies might cross the road to avoid walking past me, or people I didn't know would be a bit guarded. Now I realised why. My hair was beginning to grow back very slowly, so now I had a very fine but very short growth. Clearly, as with Gary, people had thought I was a skinhead by choice. Another lesson learnt - not to judge a book by its cover.

Things were all coming together and the list of things to do had lots of ticks on it. Cars booked, menus chosen, bridesmaids' dresses coming along with matching ties and cravats for groom, best man and ushers. Amanda's dress had been selected and flowers, photographer and now video, were all covered.

"Mark, can I have a quiet word?"

Bert was a senior associate with Grist who helped Colin with some of the merger and acquisition deals he brokered, a true old-school gent in the real sense of the word.

"Have you sorted out a honeymoon yet?"

The truth was that we hadn't. What with everything else going on and the expense of a wedding we had no great plans for a honeymoon. Our thoughts were more along the lines of a few days in Devon but nothing had been confirmed.

"No, not yet. I think we are planning on a few days away but not sure where just yet."

"Good, well Audrey and I would like to offer you our villa in Spain for two weeks. I've checked with Colin and he's happy for you to have the time off. You just need to pay for your flights to Malaga and I'll sort out a car for you and you can have the run of the place to yourselves."

"Wow. Are you sure? That's really kind of you, thank you Bert."
"That's all right. After all you've been through, I imagine a couple of weeks in the sun will do you the world of good."

"Amanda, Bert has offered us his villa in Spain for two weeks for our honeymoon!"
"You're kidding, really?"
"Yes, and a car thrown in, we just have to pay for flights."
"That's brilliant. Yes, give him a big hug from me!"

With only a week to go everything was in place. With just a tinge of 'have I remembered this' or 'who's doing that' I'd taken up a fair bit of work time being distracted by the myriad of tasks Amanda had set me and was deep in my thoughts. Colin was standing by my desk.

"We need to have a team meeting at about four o'clock, and then thought we would finish up early, about fiveish. So if you want to wrap up what you're doing and come through when you're ready."

It was ten to four; everyone else seemed to be either in Colin's office or away from their desk. It was a tradition to go for a pint on a Friday after work and this evening I had planned to meet John, my best man, along with Amanda's brothers-in-law for an informal stag do around seven.

As I walked into Colin's office, the first champagne cork popped and a small buffet appeared.

"Mark, we all just wanted to say that we've watched you come through all the events of the last year or so and we are all in awe of how you have dealt with adversity. In Amanda, you have found a wonderful, supportive girl and we all wish you both the very best for your future. To Mark."

By the time we left the office and some three pubs later, I was in an alcohol-induced 'happy' state when my work colleagues delivered me to John and the brothers-in-law to be. What they forgot to mention was that word had spread and so fellow recruitment friends and competitors were also there.

It's fair to say that these guys knew how to enjoy themselves, and by 8.30pm, I was drunk as a skunk. In my defence, I was well out of practice and adding double vodkas to a pint is just not sporting.

"Come on, let's get you home." John was doing a grand job as best man, and with a bit of help I was poured into his car. Window down, with my head hanging out like a happy dog, I was trying not to be sick inside the car. The party, I heard later, continued into the wee small hours.

Amanda had also been out with friends that evening and got home around 10.30.

"John! I didn't expect to see you."
John was happily watching our TV, with a cup of coffee in hand.
"Oh God! Is he all right? Where's Mark?" The alarm was now rising in Amanda's voice.

"He's fine, well no, he's a little the worse for wear. I've put him into bed to let him sleep it off."

"Oh my God! You were supposed to look after him! What time did you get home?"
"About quarter to nine."
"A quarter to nine! How did he get that drunk by a quarter to nine?"
"I don't know, I think the Grist guys had started early, something about a champagne reception, and then George and a few others joined us. To be fair he was quite well gone by the time I found him. Still, you're here now, so I'll leave you to it."

Amanda was seriously not impressed. The following morning I awoke with no sign of a hangover and no sign of Amanda. She had taken up residence in the spare room. I knew I was probably in trouble so made some toast and tea to present her with breakfast in bed. I'm not sure if she was more annoyed with me for getting drunk or for not showing any signs of a hangover and robbing her of the chance to say 'serves you right'.

"I think you do need a haircut."
"Are you sure?" I hadn't heard that command for such a long time. Since chemo my hair had been growing back steadily and now had a fine downy quality, but as yet since shaving the last bits off some six months earlier, I had not had a haircut and with less than a week to go before the wedding, I was a bit nervous.

"Yes, I think so. I want you to look your best, Mandy can do it here so you don't have to go to a barber. She's coming over tomorrow anyway and I want it done properly."

"OK, if you think so." So, this was payback for getting drunk.

Two days before the wedding, Amanda moved out and set up camp at Eileen's. This was it, the big day was soon upon us. I didn't really sleep the night before and so was up early; all ready and dressed, waiting for John to pick me up.

I read my horoscope in the local paper, it forewarned of terrible things but that if I held my nerve all would go well. I thought 'it can't be worse than the last year' but hoped this would be a much better period of my life. I turned my thoughts to my speech. Bugger, I should really jot something down. I'd sort of forgotten about a speech and so with half an hour to spare I jotted down three or four headers.

"All set?" John was on time.

"I think so."

"Got everything?"

"Yep."

"OK, let's go."

North Stoneham Church is a beautiful country church with just the right mix of quaint and traditional. People were arriving and chatting. I had several half conversations but was more ducklike, my calm exterior hiding the legs going ten to the dozen.

"Time to take our places, Mark." John marshalled me into the church. Guests assembled, I sat in the front pew, awaiting my bride. The organist piped up and, walking slowly, Ken led a radiant Amanda up the aisle.

As I stepped into position alongside her, our eyes met, each of us beaming broad smiles, so full of joy.

Hymns sung and vows exchanged, we were now man and wife.

Kind words from Charles; who delicately alluded to the past year and described our wedding as "a light out of the darkness".

The reception followed and now Ken was giving his speech with anecdotes of Amanda's early years and how proud he was to be representing her father. I'm sure he was there somewhere too, watching over us and smiling.

My turn to reply: with a thank-you to Ken and then to John, as best man, for getting me there in one piece. Steve heckled from the guests: "He nearly didn't make it." I turned to Amanda and back to the guests.

"Steve's right, and not just from the stag do. I proposed to Amanda just over a year ago and none of us knew what was round the corner. As most of you know I was a little bit ill, and so here, now, I want to publically give praise and say thank you to Amanda. For all of her love and support, I can truly say I would not be here without her. I once asked her how I could be sure that she loved me, her reply was, 'When you can hold a sick bowl and mop someone's brow whilst they are ill over and over again and just will them to get better, then you know you love someone.'"

I turned to Eileen; "I also want to thank Eileen. After I came out of hospital she took me in to recover, this was her chance to do me in...."

"I hadn't thought of that," Eileen chipped in.

"... and I'm grateful she didn't take the opportunity."

Speeches over, much dancing and partying followed. Finally, Amanda and I retired to our bridal suite and once we'd cleared the toothpaste from the taps, loo seat, showerhead, door handles and bedside lights, we collapsed into bed, simply holding each other in our arms. There had been many times when I had thought that we would not make it to this day, but we had, and we were here now at the end of our happiest day.

Chapter Nine

Mark

All in all, 1994 had been one hell of a year. Starting with chemotherapy, then a laparotomy and finally a wedding. Not exactly one of those years you look back on and think 'what did we do last year?' Work was stable and life began to settle down into the usual routines.

Gnawing away, at the back of my mind, a plan was beginning to form. More than anything I wanted to get myself fit again, and if I could combine this with a way of saying thank you to all the people who had helped me, then that would be a good thing.

"I want to ride from Land's End to John O'Groats."
"Are you mad? You've just had a very traumatic year, you need to recover . . . take it easy for a while."
"No, I want to do something, something significant, to raise awareness and some money for Ben and his team. This way I also get myself fit into the bargain."
"Are you sure?"

Amanda knew that I loved cycling and that in a former life I had raced but this was a bolt out of the blue and, frankly, I wasn't sure myself if I could do it. But I also knew that I would only do this if there was a weight of expectation behind me. My theory was that if I told enough people that I was going to do this, then I would simply have no choice but to buckle down and get on with it.

"OK, when do you want to do this?"

"This year, probably in the summer when the days are longer."

"How far is it anyway?"

"I'm not sure, about 750 miles I think. The non-stop record is something like two days."

"Two days! Well you're not going to do that are you! You'll need a good two weeks and August is going to be busy holiday season. I think you're mad."

We got out the atlas and tried to measure the distance using a ruler, not the most scientific but it did confirm that it was a tad more than 750 miles. After a bit of phoning around, I managed to get a copy of AutoRoute and used the computer at work to discover that it was actually 874 miles from Land's End to John O'Groats.

"Seven days."

"What?"

"Seven days for Le Jog. That's just 125 miles a day." If I said it quickly enough then it didn't seem too bad.

"Yes, each day for seven days! Mark it's too much and too soon."

"Seven days is good – it means we just need a week off work. Drive to Land's End on Friday evening, ride Saturday through to Friday and then two days to drive home. Ideal."

Amanda was not convinced that my plan was entirely watertight and to be fair neither was I, but I also knew that I had to set the bar high to make this a real challenge that I could focus on. For a whole bunch of reasons I needed a project that I could get my teeth into and getting fit was the priority.

One of our favourite films at the time was Field of Dreams starring Kevin Costner. In it was the strap line "If you build it they (he) will come", Amanda knew this and so we agreed Land's End to John

O'Groats was going to happen. I know she thought I was mad but I think she was secretly proud.

Ever since the orchidectomy some 18 months earlier, Amanda and I had attended regular follow-up clinics, mostly with Ben Mead and occasionally with one of his team. Each session followed the same routine, a blood test, chest x-ray, weight taken and then sit outside Ben's consulting room before finally being called in.

Each time Ben would shake our hands warmly and then enthusiastically share an update on the number of new patients with some anecdotal side chat. I'd then lie on the couch whilst Ben poked and prodded, checking for any unwanted lumps or bumps. We would then enter into a one-sided negotiation where Ben would say, "We'll see you in a month's time", and I would try to stretch this to two months or more.

At my last visit in November, to my surprise and delight we'd pushed the gap out to three months. So, here we were back to see Ben in February 1995. After the usual routine, we were sitting in Ben's office and he confirmed that all was on track and there was nothing untoward to report.

Amanda wasted no time.
"Mark and I have been thinking about a way we can show our appreciation to you and your team and all the work that you do. So, Mark has the idea that he would like to cycle from Land's End to John O'Groats in support of the hospital. We're thinking about doing this later this year. Would you be happy for him to do this?"

"Well, goodness, that's an admirable feat. Would I be happy for him to do this? Yes of course."

That was the response I wanted to hear.

"To be honest, I really want to do this to get myself fit again, but if it means that we can raise some awareness and some money then we would be really happy to do this."

"Oh, yes, certainly. Getting the message out there is the big thing. We've seen a tremendous rise in cases over the past few years, tremendous. Raising awareness is very important, very important." Ben's energy was obvious.

"But do you think Mark will be able to cope with it physically? Should he not be careful after such major surgery?" Amanda wanted to be sure I wasn't about to do myself any more physical damage. We were now married and she was, quite rightly, looking to protect her investment.

"Well, I should think so. It's a good thing to build up the body, especially after surgery. It's getting on for 10 months or so since Mark's last operation and there have been no complications since then. As with all these things I wouldn't recommend that you overdo it, but steady regular exercise is a good thing and cycling is a low-impact sport. We had another chap like you, he's a cyclist, had the orchidectomy and now he's back racing, so I don't foresee any problems."

"That's good to hear, doc, I'm planning on doing this in seven days which means a good 125 miles per day."

"My, that's some effort."

"So, on the money front, who should we raise money for and are there any other things we should consider? We obviously want to publicise this as much as we can."

"Well, we do have a research fund, which is used here in the hospital to help the clinical staff keep up to date with new findings. Recently we have been trialling better ways to administer chemotherapy with portable slow-release pouches, which means that patients don't need to stay in hospital so long and there is some evidence that the side effects are less traumatic. These units cost several hundred pounds each. We also use the money to attend seminars and share results with other leading research centres."

Amanda had been taken with the level of home comforts on Hamilton Fairly Ward and how these small touches had made chemo more bearable, both from the patient's point of view as well as from her perspective of feeling that I was somewhere 'nice' rather than in a drab clinical ward.

She chipped in: "We'd also like to give something to the ward directly to make things better for the people going through chemo, maybe to buy more games or something to help relieve the boredom."

I thought a hotline to KFC would do the trick.

"Yes, well Hamilton Fairly Ward also has its own fund which it uses to buy the things that are non-standard issue. All help is most gratefully received. With regards to publicity etc, we have to be very careful, especially regarding fundraising. So I need you to write to me to explain what you are planning on doing and I will make sure we get the proper authorisation."

"OK, that's good, so we are all systems go and we will raise money for both Hamilton Fairly Ward Fund and the Medical Oncology Unit Research Fund."

"Tremendous news, tremendous. Right, we'll see you back again in three months."
"Can we make it six months? I've got a lot of training to do."
"NO, three months."

"There's a bike here for sale in Poole that looks good. It's a 531 Nigel Dean hand-built frame with Shimano gears, mavic rims and quick-release hubs, only £350." I think Amanda heard 'Blah blah blah Poole blah blah blah £350.'

"You've already got a bike."

"Well, yes, but if we are going to do this properly then I need a good bike and my old one isn't really up to the job. Besides I thought we could take that as a spare just in case I have a major mechanical or something."

"£350! That sounds a lot, are you sure that this isn't just a ruse to get yourself a new bike?"

The thought hadn't crossed my mind. It might have entered my mind and stayed there but it never made it out the other side.

"Come on, you know I need decent kit if we are going to do this, don't you?"

"Well, OK, but make sure that is a good bike. I don't want you having a 'major mechanical' whatever that is, or a wheel falling off or something silly."

So, a few days later I was off to Poole and after a whizz around the block and a bit of hefty negotiation, I was now the proud owner of a Nigel Dean racing bike for £300. By now we were in March and with just six months before the 'grand depart' there was much planning and a lot of training to do.

Amanda was brilliant; organising was what she did best. Word was spreading amongst family and friends. Rowena, Amanda's sister, was especially good at championing the cause and soon we had a bank account and sponsorship forms were flying off the press.

To my amazement we were beginning to get enquiries and offers of help from people we didn't know. Our office cleaners held a charity night for us at their working men's club; gifts and bric-a-brac led to car boot sales; a couple of local bike shops provided me with clothing and spares; and Hendy Ford agreed to provide us with a car for the journey.

We were building it and they were coming!

With Amanda's previous media background she also got me a slot on the Julian Clegg radio show on BBC Radio Solent local radio and that led to a second slot to review the papers with Nick Girdler. With a briefing from Ben, each time I evangelised about testicular cancer and the importance of checking oneself, along with the great work being done right here in Southampton by Ben and his team.

The best gift and probably the most practically useful came from a friend of a friend who was a fellow cyclist who now worked for Motorola. Motorola was developing new mobile phones that didn't need a car battery to run them. These were the sort of toys that only executives used and looked as though they were straight off the USS Enterprise. We now had the full use of two for the journey.

With all this support and momentum gathering, the pressure was mounting for me to get fit enough to actually complete the ride. I had raced quite successfully as a schoolboy and junior but had stopped racing when I went to polytechnic and discovered beer and girls. I still rode the bike from time to time but never in anger and certainly not for a hundred miles at a time.

So, I was confident that the task ahead was doable but had sort of ignored the ten years of stagnation and the physical battering that comes with two rounds of surgery and four rounds of chemotherapy.

My training was not going as well as I would have liked and I knew I needed to be able to ride day-in day-out. By this time, I was now a salaried director at Grist and Colin was very much supportive of my project.

We agreed that I would take Fridays off as training time so that I could put in a long ride consecutively on Friday, Saturday and Sunday. I think Colin knew that mentally Mondays were also written off, as I would appear at my desk bleary-eyed and half asleep.

"Mother wants to come with us."
"OK?"
Eileen had been very active on the unofficial organising committee, producing all sorts of useful information on the places that we would pass through en route, but I wasn't too sure how good a navigator she would be, and if she was driving then there was a fear I would ride faster than the car.

"I need some company during the day when you are on your bike and Mother said she would like to come."

Amanda was right. She would need someone alongside, not only to navigate but also to deal with any practical issues as they arose. I had spoken to several people and one or two friends had put their names in to the hat.

"What about Alan? I thought he would be good and you could share the driving, I'm just thinking about how we would deal with a crisis if we had to."

"Well, he's all right, but I'm going to spend seven days with this person. It's all right for you. You will be out on your bike all day. I'd feel more comfortable with Mother and anyway she is very practical, you should give her more credit, she's done a lot for you and she feels involved. She wants to help."
Amanda was right again, Eileen had been a real trooper and a great

143

support right from the start, so I shouldn't be ungracious.

"Well, OK, Eileen it is then." I reasoned that should I ever think of packing in or giving up on a day, then the thought of mother-in-law and wife in the support car would give me the added incentive to stay out on the road a little longer.

Seven days had become a bit of a mantra and that was certainly my goal. However, you can only do so much training and preparation and I was still not certain that seven days would work. I had elected to go 'route one' which essentially means trying to keep as close to the original ruler line between Land's End and John O'Groats. I was still not fully confident of the actual mileage.

I was keen to stay out of towns and cities as much as I could but the direct route meant that I could not easily avoid the urban sprawl of Greater Manchester through to Lancaster and equally I elected to go through Edinburgh and then up over the Highlands to Inverness. The sensible thing would have been to stay left up to Fort William and then go along the Caledonian Canal, which would have been a much easier ride but would have added another 50 miles.

As we now had the luxury of mobile phones, we decided to work it on the fly and so rather than pre book accommodation we would take each day as it came and see how far I was going to get and then take pot luck. If we needed to, then we would always have the option of getting in the car and driving to somewhere sensible.

"Have you seen the paper?"
"Which one?"
"Both! The Echo and the Advertiser."

I'd had my name in the odd race report in Cycling Weekly but this was the first time I'd made a multi-column piece with a photo in not one but two local papers.

Amanda's final PR coup had been to get local reporters to take up my story and while they had come and taken their notes and photos I was expecting to be somewhere between 'Cat stuck up tree' and 'News in brief', if I made it in at all.

So here now I warranted a 13x2 photo and a quarter-page article in the Echo, with the headline 'Bid to bring male cancer into the open'. The Advertiser had a bigger write-up but smaller photo, each article pushing out the message about testicular cancer.

With just a week to go, the planning done, the training in the bag and kit list assembled, we were ready to roll.

Chapter Ten

Mark

Two years ago, I knew nothing of biopsies, of chemo, of cancer. Now, here I was at the Land's End Hotel, with some 800 miles ahead of me. Bike and body ready to go.

"You can't go yet! We need photos of you by the Land's End sign."

"OK, but can we get on with it? I've got a long ride ahead of me and I need to get on."

The road sign at Land's End shows John O'Groats as 875 miles away, however I had planned my route and I was sure it was only 850 or so. My plan was to aim to ride at just over 125 miles each day and complete the task in no more than seven days.

Finally, I set off along the A30, heading for Penzance. Feeling quietly confident, I aimed to keep a steady pace and wondered how long it would be before Amanda and Eileen caught me up.

Soon enough I had reached Penzance, with the helicopter to the Scilly Isles taking off right in front of me. Now the road was getting busier and wider. A couple more hours and Bodmin came and went. The traffic jammed up as a car crash ahead had blocked the road. I rode around the damaged cars without giving them a second thought. Some way behind, my support crew were trying to work the phone to check I wasn't the victim.

Then, up and on to the moors, the A30 carving a wide dragon's back-like scythe across the bleak landscape. Virtually straight but up and down over ever growing larger rolling hills. The wind was getting stronger with nothing to break its path. A day that had started full of optimism and expectation was now becoming a battle. And this was only day one!

By mid-afternoon the phones were on and Amanda and Eileen were looking for some serious shopping time before finding the first night's accommodation. With Oakhampton in sight and some 90 miles covered we had to decide whether to stop or push on. The day's ride was getting harder and harder but I was determined to stay on schedule, so we pushed on.

"Where are you?" The signal was faint and to be honest I wasn't sure where I was. I had pulled off the main road at the junction that Amanda had described, but having covered 110 miles of relentless, wind-swept, up-and-down dual carriageway I could barely tell you my name, let alone which part of Devon or Cornwall I was in.

After several moments checking the map we agreed on where I was; but I still had no idea where they were, other than it was a very nice B&B. At that moment I would have killed for a warm bath and some hot food but scarcely had the will to live. To add to my woes it was now getting dark.

"We'll come and get you . . . just stay there."

The great thing about riding a long and hard ride is that once you stop, 'just staying there' is a very simple task.

The car headlights shone in my face. As I peered through the gloom I could make out Amanda in the passenger seat.
"Hi," I whimpered, an overwhelming sense of relief that very soon I would be in a hot bath, fed and then to bed.

When I woke the next morning, my legs felt heavy - from the efforts of the previous day. The smell of bacon was just enough to lure me out of bed and into the shower.

"How are you feeling this morning? Your poor bits cycling all that way." Eileen had a way with words that conveyed just the right amount of concern, wrapped with in a healthy dose of 'you must be mad'.

"Fine thank you, Eileen. That should be the worst bit over with. The roads should be better from here on until we reach Scotland."

Scotland! This was just the morning of day two. We were still in Devon, my legs felt like lead and my body was screaming. Don't talk just eat, man. Scotland seemed a very long way away.

Breakfast over, I checked my bike and set off up the long drive and on to the road heading towards Bristol, leaving Amanda and Eileen behind to pack up leisurely and settle the bill.

The day before I had set off from Land's End with great expectation, full of hope and enthusiasm for the trip ahead. I had averaged just over 14mph for the day, covering some 110 miles. Now, this morning, I was crawling along the road, struggling to muster 10 or 11 miles per hour. With every stroke of the pedals my legs shouted back 'not again!'

"Hiya! Are you going far?" The camaraderie of fellow cyclists is legendary and here this morning was a gift from the gods.

"John O'Groats." Not the reply he was expecting.

"Bloody hell, tuck in then . . ."

My companion was a local club cyclist out on a training run. Hearing of my quest, he happily took the lead and, with all my track cycling experience coming into play, I hung on to his rear wheel like toffee. Soon we were bowling along at 18 to 20 miles per hour and the tired legs gave way to warmed-up muscles and a reinvigorated Mark.

"We thought we'd missed you!"
"Well I wasn't hanging about. What time did you leave the B&B?"
"Not that long after you, we just finished breakfast, packed and were on our way, so about an hour or so after you."

"I think it might be a good idea to make it a bit shorter today. Let's get through Bristol and then see how I feel."

Two bananas later, I was back on the road, the girls heading off to Bristol hoping to find the shops before I got too close.

As I pulled into the Travel Lodge on the outskirts of Gloucester, I was pleased that this was the end of day two. I had a dull glow over my whole body but nothing like the near exhaustion of day one. Well worth treating myself to a pint of beer and a well-earned steak and chips.

Day three was a relatively event-free day, well event-free for me. We had had some fun getting a signal on the phones and battery life was at a premium. So, as I wound my way up the quiet A-roads through Worcester, Bridgnorth, Telford and Whitchurch, Amanda and Eileen went in search of a car charger for the phone.

Now sorted out, they set about getting ahead of me and phoning around for our night's accommodation. We had settled into a routine where I would set off, they would pack up and catch me on the road usually around elevenses. The girls would then press on for a bit of sightseeing or shopping or lunch, before catching me again mid-afternoon when they would phone ahead to book a room before calling me to let me know the day's destination.

Today's target was Warrington. Now, it was getting late in the day and Warrington was just up the road with no news from the girls. I'd covered just shy of 120 miles and had pulled up outside an independent travel lodge motel called Tall Trees, just south of Warrington.

"Where are you?"
"Heading towards Liverpool."
"What the hell are you doing going to Liverpool?"
"We were trying to find a Travel Lodge on the M62 and took a wrong turning. It's all right; we know where we are now. We should be able to turn round at the next junction. Where are you?"
"I'm outside a motel, just south of Warrington. This looks fine, shall I see if they have rooms?"
"We've booked the other one but we'll have to come back to get you which might take an hour."
"I'm not going on a motorway! Hold on, I'll check here."

So armed with emergency credit card and mobile phone, the road weary, dishevelled cyclist presented himself at reception.

"Hi, do you have two rooms for tonight?"
"Yes, certainly. Twins or doubles?" The receptionist was looking around for the rest of my party.
"One of each should be fine." I explained they were on their way.

"I've booked two rooms, it's the Tall Trees lodge, Tarporley, just south of Warrington. The keys are in reception, I'm off to have a bath."
"What about your bike?"
"It's fine, I'm taking it into the room."

At this point I wasn't sure if I was sharing a room with just the bike or Amanda. Thankfully, we all saw the funny side once when we were reunited, helped by my friend Andy who lived not too far away and had dropped over for a beer and to tell us stories of other motorists lost in the M62 triangle.

Day four and this was the bit I was least looking forward to. I'd tried to stay in the countryside as much as I could, but this next section was pretty much unavoidable urban jungle, right the way through from Warrington to Preston. Going was slow, with no real chance to gather momentum.

"Hi, I'm not going to make Preston by 10.30 - 11 at best."
"OK. There's a McDonald's just south of Preston, we'll meet you there."

At 11.30, I pulled into McDonald's for a welcome and much-needed Big Mac. Already behind schedule, I pressed on towards Lancaster. Having missed a planned rendezvous at the rail station, I was pleased to see the support team overtake me on the road. They pulled over into a dusty lorry park. As I drew alongside, Amanda wound down the window and the waft of KFC gently caressed my nostrils. Tuesday was obviously takeaway day.

"Ahh . . . good move." As I reached in to take a piece of chicken.
"Hands off! This is our lunch, you had a Big Mac."
"That's not fair! I'm the one burning calories."
"Well, OK, but don't blame me if you get indigestion."

Back on the road, restocked with drink and fruit, our target for the day was Penrith. This meant that the toughest climb of the journey lay ahead. So, after my final tea stop of the day in Kendal, I began the 10-mile climb up Shap Hill, which rises from 100ft above sea level in Kendal to some 1,400ft at its peak.

At the top, Amanda and Eileen were waiting and had met another group supporting a three-man team also riding from Land's End to John O'Groats. They were raising money in support of motor neurone sufferers. Sensibly, they were taking 10 days and going via Fort William. We gratefully shared hot tea from their camper van and then pressed on for the 15 miles of downhill into Penrith.

I'd set off at 8.30am that morning and now it was just gone 6.30pm when I pulled into the B&B. It had been a very long day with of two very different halves. Land's End was already a world away.

That evening we took stock of the journey so far. It was becoming clear that seven days might be a tad ambitious. So far I'd covered some 460-odd miles and so we were just over half way. To be on target I needed to be 40 miles up the road.

"Looking at the map, I think Scotland is going to be more difficult to find places to stay, especially out of towns."

"I think you're right, and you've done a lot riding over the last four days. We don't have to do this in seven days, eight days may be more sensible and enjoyable."

Amanda was right; realistically an eighth day was now inevitable. On one hand, I was disappointed; seven days had been my mantra for a long time and I didn't like the thought of giving up on it. On the other hand, I felt a real sense of relief passing through me. I was getting into a rhythm and very was confident that I could cover 400 miles over four days without any grief.

"I'm worried about the Forth Road Bridge, and not sure I want to do that at the end of a long day, let alone fighting my way across Edinburgh in rush hour. I think we should aim for the southern outskirts and find somewhere there."

"How far is that?"

"About 100 miles or so. It will be good to have an 'easier' day with a bit less pressure."

8.30am - this was day five, ahead of us lay Scotland and the next stop was Edinburgh.

On the road out of Penrith, heading up to Carlisle, I caught up with the motor neurone trio. We rode along together for a couple of miles until I pushed on leaving them to stay left and to Fort William, while I headed right on to the A7 towards the Lowlands. Crossing the Scottish border and leaving England behind, it struck me that there was still a long way to go and Scotland was a lot bigger than I had thought.

The Lowlands were just beautiful, with very few roads and even less traffic. With the pressure off a bit, I was getting into a comfortable steady pace. Up ahead of me, here in the middle of nowhere was a fellow cyclist - well an old man on a bike, to be fair. His bike was as old as he was, and kitted out in shabby tweeds, man and bike were an incredible sight. I rolled past him with a simple "Hiya" as I carried on my way, wondering where he could have come from.

Lost in my thoughts a few miles later and now climbing one of many inclines, I heard a deep Billy Connolly-esc voice behind me.

"Green tyres! Who the hell rides on green tyres?"
The thick accent took some deciphering and, as I was working it out, the man pulled alongside.
"Where do you get green tyres young man? I've never seen green tyres."

I was stunned. Here was the old man I'd passed some miles back, who not only had caught me but was now riding a crate of rust faster than me uphill.

"They came with the bike. Do you like them?"

"Noo, I don't."

And with that, he slipped behind never to be seen again. Had he really chased me for a couple of miles just to express his amazement at my tyres? And how had he caught me? I was doing 17 to 20mph.

After a tea stop in Hawick, I continued on through Selkirk, Galashiels and onward towards Edinburgh. Lost in my thoughts, I realised that most of my knowledge of Scottish geography came from listening to the football results.

Booking accommodation over the phone can sometimes be hit and miss, and as I pulled into the Laird and Dog in Lasswade, my first impression was not good; a dark and drab wayside pub, due for renovation 100 years earlier.

There was a collective of curmudgeonly old men in the bar and Amanda and Eileen were sitting in a corner, drinking coffee.

"Hello, you made good time," Amanda, pleased to see me.

"Yes… This is an interesting place."

"It's fine really, Gordon, the landlord, is really helpful."

"You must be Mark. I hear you have had quite a journey, welcome to the Laird and Dog."

"Yes thanks, I guess you're Gordon."

"Aye."

"Is there anywhere I can work on my bike? I just need to do some running repairs."

"Yes of course, you can use the stock room. And you can leave your bike there overnight, it will be safer there. Do you need any tools? If so just give us a shout."

Running repairs meant taking the bottom bracket apart, greasing and reassembling it, followed by tightening up the brake and gear cables. While I worked, Gordon and I chatted about the ride and why I was doing it.

Later, after a wash and brush up, Eileen, Amanda and I made our way went down to the bar to eat; by now it was 8 o'clock. The chef had stayed on for us and a hearty steak and kidney pie was the selected choice.

After we had eaten, Gordon came over to our table.
"We've had a bit of a whip-round for you, there's about £50 for you to put it the pot."

We looked across to the bar; the 'curmudgeonly old men' were tipping their 'wee heavies' in acknowledgement. That night my mind was full of thoughts: the old building was unnerving me, I was wondering if the place was haunted; the kindness of strangers; not to judge a book by its cover; how far I had come; what I had gone through with chemo; who was that old man on the road?

Once again after a hearty breakfast, I was back on the road and now working my way through Edinburgh to the Forth Road Bridge. I was fairly sure you could cycle across but just in case I had arranged to meet Amanda and Eileen at the start of the crossing.

Photo opportunities taken, I set off on the bridge cycle path, a separate track, slung to the side of the road carriageway. The wind was picking up, pushing me toward the edge. A fantastic view and a great experience but I was happy to reach the other side.

Onward towards Perth, the scenery was stunning, the wind had died down and the sun was out. A car passed by which looked vaguely familiar, a bit like Dad's, surely not? As I came into the outskirts of Perth I was riding along a wonderful, wide, tree-lined boulevard. The phone rang; I'd perfected the art of answering the phone while riding, so whipped it out of my back pocket still rolling down the road.

"Hi, I'm just coming into Perth, where are you?"
"We're in a tea shop opposite the information centre. You can't miss it, there's a man playing bagpipes outside."
"OK. I'll see you in five to ten minutes."

As I put the phone in my back pocket, I noticed a young couple who had stopped walking along the path and were just watching me. Immediately, from behind a tree, Dad leapt out into the road, camera ready paparazzi-style. I swerved slightly to avoid him and, not stopping, I shouted back: "We're in the tea shop on the high street. See you there."

The young couple continued to watch as this unfolded in front of them. I could imagine them wondering who was that person cycling, with mobile phone and people taking pictures. Was he famous? I half expected them to turn up at the tea shop. Mum and Dad, on the other hand, I wasn't expecting at all.

The final leg of the day took us into Blair Atholl, just off the A9. To my surprise there was no sign of Amanda and Eileen. The girls had stopped in Pitlochry at the information centre to find a good B&B. Booked one, called me to let me know, and then driven off with the phone on the roof. Luckily, the phone survived and was still there when they parked up to go shopping further along the main road.

The start of day seven saw me facing the second big climb of the tour. Mostly on the cycle path beside the A9, up through the pass of Drumochter and on to Dalwhinnie and the ski resorts of the Cairngorms.

We were deep into whisky country and I think the fumes were luring Eileen. As I was going to be spending the next three hours climbing, Eileen was keen to take the opportunity to tour the nearby Bell's distillery.

The A9 is a notoriously bad road and, true to form, a bad accident had blocked the road. On the cycle path, I was unaffected but, remembering back to day one, I thought it best to call in. The girls caught up with me on the top, and after a brief stop to refuel with drinks and a banana, they went off to Aviemore for fish and chips and I pressed on to Inverness.

Now the roads were good and the mostly downhill stretch meant that I was making up for the slow start to the day. After a quick call, I decided to press on and not stop at Inverness, keen to make my last day as short as possible. We settled on Tain, and Amanda and Eileen made the best of it with afternoon tea and shopping in Inverness.

The scenery continued to impress, with the bridges over Beauly and Cromarty Firths an altogether different experience from the heavy Forth Road Bridge. Eventually I reached Tain with 115 miles covered and just 86 to go.

At Tain, we stayed in the Golf View Guesthouse, with wonderful views out across the Dornoch Firth, where oil rigs were being built or were in for maintenance. At the end of each day's ride I would have a soak in the bath and, since reaching Scotland, the baths were increasingly bigger. Today's bath must have been a good 7ft long! I floated stretched out full length and was still not touching the ends - I'd come too far to drown in the bath!

Just one more day to go.

Chapter Eleven
Mark

Day eight, my last day in the saddle, and ahead of me the rugged coast road up to John O'Groats. The weather forecast predicted rain and heavy winds; I didn't care, this was the final leg of my journey.

The first (and last) tea stop was at Helmsdale, roughly half way. We stopped at La Mirage, a quite incredible café full of entertainment memorabilia and pictures of famous patrons. It was amazing to find such a place so far from anywhere.

Pushing on, we agreed to rendezvous again further up the coast at Dunbeath, which seemed the most likely place to have a café. When I got there, Amanda and Eileen were waiting in the old harbour. The place was deserted. I was damp from earlier showers and so, with a steep climb in front of me, I decided not to hang around.

The girls went on to the Caithness Glass factory, just outside Wick, for a cup of tea.
Eileen, looking out of the window: "Is that Mark? Already?"
"Yes! Come on! We've got to go! Leave your tea. He can't get to the end before us."

I'd ridden myself fit over the past seven days and now, with less than 20 miles to go, safe in the knowledge that I didn't need to hold back I was flying.

"Arrgh . . . It won't start!"

"Calm down, dear, you don't want to flood the engine."

Arrgh . . . We haven't come this far not to be at the finish! Come on! Start! Damn you!"

"Shall I call the RAC?" Eileen was trying to keep calm in a crisis. Amanda was far from calm and rapidly becoming the crisis.

"At last! Come on, we've got to catch him!"

The car, which had behaved perfectly all week, had decided now was a good time to play up. Finally bursting into life, Amanda breathed a huge sigh of relief and with a red mist firmly in place, set out rally style in the race to John O'Groats.

Meanwhile, I had no idea they were behind me and was somewhat surprised by the tooting horn as they passed me with some five miles to go. As they raced to the finish, my mind began to take in the enormity of the journey we had all been on.

Two years and 25 days earlier:

"Go to the doctor!"

I knew Amanda was right but the thought of going to the doctor filled me with dread.

"Go to the doctor!"

There it was again, she wasn't going to take "No" for an answer.

"Mark I'm serious; you should have these things checked out."

Of course Amanda was right. What If I'd left things a while, where would I be now? Would I be here at all? It wasn't a thought I wanted to dwell on.

Thinking of chemo, how after round one I thought 'this was a piece of cake'. How chemo won rounds two and three, dealing some hefty blows. Of endlessly being sick, over and over again, of hospital food, of wobbly jelly! A smile came back to my face; wobbly jelly just does that to you.

Here I was, feeling fitter than I had in a long while, thinking back to the days of climbing stairs one at a time, of walking round the block looking and feeling like an old man.

Thinking back to then, I could never have imagined the me now riding along at 20 mph, the wind behind me, a hand pushing me along. My darkest hour, putting my hand in the hand of God; I gripped the handlebars a little tighter. I'm not letting go just yet!

Memories of the nurse who had made me tea that first night I was sick, and the simple human kindness she had shown. Of Dr Bamber and Mr Smart, and their decisiveness which put me on the road to recovery.

Of the friends and family who had been touched by what they saw, my brother and his family who didn't know what to say. Of work colleagues who felt awkward. "Don't feel awkward!", I heard myself say.

I thought about the ride from Land's End and the significance of wanting to prove I wasn't beaten. How Eileen always had a smile, always with a turn of phrase, and always by Amanda's side.

The impact Ben Mead had had on my life and the massive respect for a man so enthusiastically doing his bit to save lives. Understanding that I was just one of many patients but I was always made to feel important. Ben was the important one, no question.

And to Amanda, my rock, for the times she must have despaired, for the anguish of watching me suffer, for the tears unseen and for simply putting up with me.

Ahead I could see the welcoming committee, Amanda and Eileen by the John O'Groat's sign, bottle of bubbly at the ready, cheering as I approached.

I just beamed with wave after wave of emotion. We had all come on a journey. Each and every one of us with our own part to play, and our own tale to tell. Not one of us was unscarred. In that moment, I fully appreciated that life and living is truly a team effort.

We had raised £1,500 for Hamilton Fairley Ward Fund and a further £5,120 for the Medical Oncology Unit Research Fund. Money we knew would be well spent and was well deserved.

Now our journey was complete – it was time to go home.